THE ANATOMY OF BELIEF AND UNBELIEF

Ian Walker

Thomas & Mercer

For JB
Muse, thaumaturge, companion, my love

'Lord, I believe; help thou my unbelief.'
Mark 9.24

CONTENTS

FOREWORD

This is a polemical book. I do not always argue my conclusions. I have done that elsewhere (see my *Faith and Belief: A Philosophical Approach,* The American Academy of Religion, Atlanta, 1994, et al.). I mean to provoke serious consideration of the nature of religious belief, particularly in the Christian tradition, and of unbelief, particularly agnosticism and atheism.

My contention is that most people, wrongly, see religious belief in propositional terms, i.e., as being expressed as propositions - say, the statements of the creeds - that are true or false, or have some degree of probability attaching to them. This wrong-headed view can only be seen to apply to the historical tenets, which may be defeasible, at the core of religion (chapter 1).

A brief examination of the history of early Christianity reveals that discovering anything about, say, the life of Jesus (or Abraham, or Mohammed, or ...), unembellished by faith, is impossible (chapters 2-4).

Attempts to recover the life of Jesus are examined and found to end in relative failure (chapters 5-6).

Moreover, such attempts are quite recent and do not represent faith through the ages (chapter 7).

I offer a brief consideration of some errors of propositional belief, together with some thoughts on the value of myth (chapters 8-9).

Taking one of the world's principal apologists for propositional belief - Richard Swinburne, Emeritus Professor of Philosophy at Oxford University - I show how his reliance on the use of evidence in religion is flawed (chapter 10).

In chapter 11, I offer a little light relief.

Belief, in historical terms at least, is best understood as faith, which is itself a virtue, like hope or love or justice; it is not a set of propositional beliefs (chapter 12).

But is historical certainty necessary anyway? Does faith depend upon the veracity of certain historical propositions? I examine this question by reference to the work of Lessing, Kierkegaard and William James, and conclude that faith is indeed a virtue, as Socrates would have it (chapter 13).

I then attempt to show that, even if belief were principally propositional, it is not without insuperable difficulties. I do this by means of an examination of miracles; one such - the resurrection - lies at the heart of Christian belief (chapter 14).

Having considered belief, I then turn my attention to unbelief: firstly, to agnosticism (chapter 15), where I attempt to demonstrate that, if viewed propositionally (as *ex hypothesi* it must be), agnosticism is not without fatal intellectual flaws. I then consider atheism in four possible guises and discover that, not only does atheism often misrepresent the real nature of faith, but that it, too, is not without serious shortcomings (chapter 16).

I then address the question of ethics and consider whether there can be a religious ethics (chapter 17).

Finally, I consider death in an attempt to show that the metaphysical features which accompany propositional belief are misleading and inappropriate (chapter 18).

Ian Walker
Oxon, 2023

1
What is belief?

Nowadays, belief is largely construed as propositional. This, 'propositional', is a technical term in modern logic; it means: what is asserted when a sentence is used to say something true or false[1]. Propositions are the sense of sentences. Propositional belief is saying of one proposition that it is more likely than another; that it is probable. More often than not, religious belief is seen, at least in common parlance, in this way.

But there is more to belief than a propositional attitude: to believe in truth, justice and the American way, is to exercise trust or a commitment rather than to believe that it is probable that such things exist or are true, rather than that they do not exist or are false. I do not refer here to the hackneyed 'believing in' *contra* 'believing that' dichotomy. As we shall see below, I am thinking mainly of belief with a personal object.

The relationship that holds between a person and a proposition she believes is not unproblematical: when I *know*, *remember* or *discover* a proposition then the truth of that proposition is entailed. One cannot be said to *know* that the earth is flat unless the earth is, in fact, flat.

But *believes* functions differently: while one can be said to believe a proposition, one cannot hope or fear a proposition. And to know a proposition is different from knowing its truth.

In this sense, *believes* functions more like: *doubts, asserts, denies, proves, affirms*, than it does like *understands, knows, remembers, considers*. Some of these intentional verbs express attitudes to truth in a way that others do not. Failure to understand this simple equivocation, as we shall see, leads to misunderstandings in respect of faith, belief and unbelief.

Belief expresses an attitude to truth in a way which not all similar attitudes to propositions do. And this attitude to truth is today usually expressed as epistemic probability: it is based on the probability of a proposition relative to its evidence; that is, the total evidence available.

It may be that I believe the proposition p on the basis of evidence formulable as q, r and s which in turn I believe on the basis of x, y and z and so on; this could be seen to issue in an infinite regress. But there comes a point where one's beliefs hit what Wittgenstein calls 'bedrock': a place where propositions are so anchored in one's experience of the world that they are not made probable by other propositions. 'I see my wife watering the garden' is one such. I am inclined to believe this, not because I believe something else, but because my experience of the world forces it upon me.

Religion and Propositional Belief

As we shall see, it is most common that religious belief is construed, mistakenly, as propositional belief. But is there a place in the life of religion where propositional belief may be correctly identified? Inasmuch as religion has a history and intends past events then it is defeasible; it is open to the machinations of historians; it can be shown to be false. All religions make just such corrigible, historical claims but these must be approached with caution. Bornkamm is correct in believing that 'mathematical certainty in the exposition of a bare history of Jesus, unembellished by faith, is unobtainable'[2]. The same is true of a 'bare history' of Abraham, Siddhartha Gautama or Mohammed. As we shall see, we must tread carefully when appraising defeasible events intended as core, historical tenets of a religion.

Doubtless the crucifixion and resurrection of Jesus lie at the heart of Christian belief. Yet St Paul, *pace* the Evangelists, did not believe in a bodily resurrection.

St Paul, who invented Christianity and wrote much of the New Testament (although not all he is generally credited with) was, perversely, probably an early Christian Gnostic[3]. It is an irony of great moment that Christians today unknowingly commit to a sectarian, radical version of Christianity which was, by the Council of Nicaea (AD 325), innocently and ignorantly adopted as orthodoxy. Christians are all, unwittingly, Pauline Gnostics now, although tensions remain, in the New Testament itself and in Christians today, between Gnostics and anti-Gnostics.

I shall look briefly at the historicity of the life of Jesus to consider its defeasibility.

Notes:

1. I see no point in becoming involved in the technical issue of whether the Fregean sense employed here is correct, i.e., to consider the distinction between semantic meaning and speaker meaning. I am happy, for simplicity's sake, to stick with the *Oxford Companion to Philosophy*'s: 'a proposition ... is customarily defined as "what is asserted" when a sentence ... is used to say something true or false ...'
2. p.14, *Jesus of Nazareth*, Hodder and Stoughton, 1969. Cf. E.P. Sanders, p. 73, *The Historical Figure of Jesus*: 'There are no sources that give us the "unvarnished truth"; the varnish of faith in Jesus covers everything.'
3. See Chapter 3 below.

2
A Life of Jesus

The principal elements, identified in the Gospels, of a life of Jesus (Paul is not much interested in Jesus' life), could be summarised as:

-       baptism by John the Baptist
-       itinerant ministry leading to:
-       the Passion:
    - triumphal entry to Jerusalem
    - last supper, Gethsemane
    - arrest
    - trial – Peter's denial - Pilate's condemnation
    - crucifixion
    - burial
    - resurrection (although not in Mark)

Extra-biblical sources for Jesus' life are scant (at least, as seen in modern terms): the notoriously unreliable Flavius Josephus (c. AD 37 – c. 100) – it is sometimes thought that all references to Jesus in Josephus are third century Christian interpolations, although, interestingly, that references to John the Baptist are genuine; two snippets from Suetonius (c. AD 69 – c. 140); Tacitus (c. AD 56 to 117); Pliny the Younger (c. AD 62 – c. 113); apocryphal and Gnostic sources; Rabbinic sources; extensive references in the – later – Church Fathers (the earliest Apostolic Fathers date from the late first and early second centuries).

It is safe to say that Jesus was an itinerant preacher, probably a disappointed eschatologist, who fell foul of the Roman and Jewish authorities in Jerusalem where he was crucified c. AD 30. His principal message was: *The Kingdom of Heaven is at hand. Repent and prepare.* Indeed, his message was not what we think of today as the Christian message; those are later accretions for which the apostle Paul is largely responsible.

We can discount fanciful apocryphal and gnostic stories which claim he escaped crucifixion and lived to an old age in retirement, or, that he escaped crucifixion, married and had children or, etc.

Of course, the most contentious episode in Jesus' life is the resurrection. And part of the difficulty here is that the resurrection accounts in the Bible are full of contradictions and inconsistencies, but these have nothing to do with any uncertainty about the resurrection faith. On the contrary, they represent varying attempts to give that faith expression.

The only undoubtedly early tradition that speaks of the resurrection in any detail is that in 1 *Corinthians* 15 (undoubtedly written by St Paul) and there, we find, not a description but a list of appearances which tells us nothing of the resurrection, except that it occurred, and nothing of the empty tomb or of the nature of the appearances listed.

One thing that is clear, however, is that Paul saw his own experience, along with that of the other witnesses he lists, as God's revelatory act. And it is possible, if not likely, that this revelatory act was construed by him as an eschatological event, seen in terms of Jewish apocalyptic. The Lukan timespan of forty days for the post-resurrection appearances is theologically motivated and historically unreliable; there are reasons to consider that reports of appearances may have extended over a period of years. Some elements of the Pauline list were dropped from the tradition of later years for reasons on which we can only speculate.

The speeches of the *Acts of the Apostles* which refer to the resurrection are neither reliable nor early. It seems likely that they do not represent the earliest stratum of tradition, as was once popularly held.

The next early tradition is to be found in *Mark*, but there we do not find post-resurrection appearances, even though we do find the empty tomb that is absent in Paul. The empty tomb tradition is not likely to be the evangelist's but we cannot assess how far back behind *Mark* it goes. Even here, however, it is the angelophany, and not the empty tomb, which awakens faith. There are reasons to conclude that the empty tomb tradition, even in its earliest available form in *Mark*, is historically unreliable.

Christophanies represent a later strand of tradition which are just beginning in *Matthew* (with, possibly, a somewhat early form in *John* 20:15 ff) but here it is not clear whether the Christophanies are of the Exalted One from heaven, or of a more earthly nature; probably the former.

The latest biblical strata of development are to be found in *Luke* 24 and *John* 20 where the Christophanies take the form of the revelation of a 'Divine Man'. Here apologetic motifs have taken a firm foothold and account for the stress on the corporeality of the resurrected Jesus. In later strata still, notably the apocryphal and gnostic writings, the apologetic emphases become predominant and the expansion of the narrative is complete.

The general trend of the traditions then is from revelatory appearances (to be distinguished from later Christophanies) to the historically unreliable empty tomb, to corporeal Christophanies. The development of the tradition in roughly this manner accounts for the inconsistencies and contradictions in the accounts. And there are good reasons why we should doubt the historical accuracy of some of the later strands of tradition, for example, that Jesus ate fish (*John* 21: 1-14; *Luke* 24: 42-43), or the physical touch of the Thomas story (*John* 20: 24-29), or the Emmaus encounter (*Luke* 24: 13-32). First, these motifs are entirely absent in the earliest round of tradition and, indeed, do not fit easily with these traditions: for example, the idea of an exalted, heavenly, non-corporeal, resurrected Lord eating grilled fish is something of a nonsense. Secondly, there are good reasons (e.g., apologetical and liturgical, etc.) to account for these later developments. Thirdly, these later strata of tradition represent more the church's attempts at understanding the implications of the resurrection than they represent a witness to it.

Was it the case that the faith of the primitive church was based on data whose conclusions can only be offered in probabilistic terms? No. The 'evidence', such as it is, is so inextricably linked with the confession of the early church that no such deductions are possible. As Dibelius says: 'The mythological element takes charge of the entire material of evangelical history.'[1]

Here we find ourselves caught in the distinction between the Jesus of history and the Christ of faith which lies at the root of such academic phenomena as *The Quest for the Historical Jesus*.

It would seem that in the only area where belief

might correctly be construed in propositional terms, in offering probabilities, we are thwarted: we simply cannot know. Again, Dibelius:

'Whatever was told of Jesus' words and deeds was always a testimony of faith as formulated for preaching and exhortation in order to convert unbelievers and confirm the faithful. What founded Christianity was not knowledge about a historical process, but the confidence that the content of the story was salvation: the decisive beginning of the End.'[2]

It was up to St Paul – and to a lesser extent, the Church Fathers of the second century onwards – to superimpose on the bare eschatological bones of Jesus' teaching the infrastructure we now have come to think of as Christian belief. It was St Paul who fleshed out Jesus' apocalyptic message, accommodating it to the ever-longer-than-expected wait for the Last Days, and who instituted the decisive break from eschatological Judaism, pushing the newly-fledged faith into the pagan world.

Notes:
1. p. 288, *From Tradition to Gospel,* Ivor Nicholson and Watson, 1934.
2. *op. cit.* p.295.

3
The Gnostic Paul[1]

About 2300 BC, in the sixth Egyptian dynasty, the mountain of Jabal al-Tarif near the town of Nag Hammadi was riddled with over 150 natural limestone caves. These caves were painted and extended and used for the burial of the dead.

In December 1945, Muhammad ʻAli al-Samman and his brothers went to Jabal on their camels in search of *sabakh,* a fertiliser much-prized in that area. As they dug around a boulder, they struck a large, red, earthenware jar. They were reluctant to break the jar to discover its contents, fearing it might contain a *jinn*, or evil spirit. As they were about to avenge their father's murder in a blood feud, such an action would have been inauspicious.

Considering also that the jar might contain treasure, Muhammad's greed overcame his fear and he smashed the jar open and found it contained thirteen papyrus books. Little did he realise that his discovery was far more valuable than the gold he coveted or Howard Carter's discovery of Tutankhamen's tomb on 26 November, 1922.

Muhammad took the books home, leaving them on the straw near his mother's oven. His mother,

'Umm-Ahmad, used some of the papyrus to kindle her fire.

Three weeks later, Muhammad and his brothers avenged their father's death by killing Ahmed Isma'il: they hacked off his limbs, ripped out his heart and ate it. Fearful that the police investigating Ahmed's murder would search his house and discover the strange books, he asked the priest al-Qummus Basiliyus Abd al-Masih to look after them. Al-Qummus Basiliyus showed the books to Raghib, a friend who taught history, who believed they might be valuable; he sent one book to a friend in Cairo to see if this was so.

The Egyptian authorities became suspicious when the books were sold on the black market; they confiscated ten and a half of the leather-bound books, bought another and put them in the Coptic Museum in Cairo.

Most of one volume, the thirteenth, was smuggled out of Egypt and put up for sale in America. When he heard of the sale, Prof Gilles Quispel, an historian of religion at the University of Utrecht in the Netherlands, bought the book with cash supplied by the Jung Foundation in Zürich.

On finding that some pages were missing, he flew to Cairo in the spring of 1955 and went straight to the Coptic Museum. There he obtained photographs of some of the texts and took them back to his hotel room to translate them. He was

shocked at the first line he read:
'These are the secret words which the living Jesus spoke, and which the twin, Judas Thomas, wrote down. Whoever finds the meaning of these sayings will not taste death' (*Gospel of Thomas* 32:10 – 11).

The Gospel of Thomas was one of 52 texts discovered by Muhammad Ali al-Samman at Nag 'Hammadi. Muhammad later admitted that he had burned or thrown away some of the texts. What remains is one of the greatest discoveries of the last century: mainly Christian writing dating back over 1500 years, including a collection of previously unknown early Christian gospels. The originals, of which the Nag 'Hammadi library is a Coptic translation, date to the second half of the first century. In other words, they are earlier than or contemporary with the New Testament gospels *Matthew, Mark, Luke* and *John*.

The Nag 'Hammadi texts were written by Christians known as Gnostics (Greek: *gnosis* = knowledge).

Before the discovery of the Nag 'Hammadi texts, New Testament scholars generally thought that St Paul was an opponent of the Gnostic heresy (Greek: *hairesis*, properly = choice). Gnosticism is a generic term covering dozens of rival theosophical sects whose adaptations of Christianity led to schism with the primitive church between c. AD 80 and

200.

Harnack saw Gnosticism as an 'acute Hellenization of Christianity' but its dualism is far more Oriental than Greek: it offers an alternative to an eschatological view of history; redemption by other means.

Predating Christianity, it contains elements drawn from pagan syncretism, Platonism, Hellenized Zoroastrianism and Judaism. In short, according to Lietzmann, 'the mysticism of the orient is added to philosophical pantheism'[2].

Essentially, Gnostics contended that we are divine sparks imprisoned in matter. The world of matter is alien to a Supreme God and to goodness, and all this is clothed in aetiological myth and ridiculous cosmologies. Salvation consists in sloughing off matter through the exercise of secret knowledge – hence 'Gnosticism' – to be incorporated into the Supreme Godhead; it is a religion of redemption from the material. As John Gray says, it is a belief whereby 'humans can be delivered from a dark world by the saving light of knowledge'[3].

A variant of Gnosticism is Docetism (Greek: *dokein* = to seem) which took Gnosticism to its logical conclusion: the belief that matter is inherently evil becomes, in Docetism, the idea that Christ's incarnation was only an appearance, a semblance. (It is interesting that the *Qur'an*, speaking of Jesus, says that the Jews 'did not kill him, nor did they crucify him, though it was made to appear like that (or a semblance) to them' (4:157)).

According to pre-Nag 'Hammadi scholars, St Paul writes his letters, in part, to refute the claims of Gnostics to 'secret wisdom'. There are good reasons now for believing this view to be false.

Second century Gnostic writers adopt St Paul's writing as a primary source for Gnostic thinking. The most influential of the Gnostic sects, the Valentinians, avow him as a Gnostic initiate. Marcion, albeit an idiosyncratic Gnostic, held St Paul in 'profound reverence' and interpreted Paul's teaching about the supersession of the Old Testament law by the Gospel to mean that the Old Testament had no authority for the Christian.

Allusions to Scripture in the *Gospel of Truth*, probably by Valentinus and doctrinally unparalleled in contemporary Hellenistic literature, demonstrate 'how profound is the Pauline influence' (J. Menard). So, too, the *Epistle to Rheginos* and elsewhere, where the development of a wide range of Pauline themes is evident: the relation of God to the elect; baptism as 'dying with Christ'; Paul's teaching on the resurrection; his exhortation on participation in the body of Christ[4].

Now while it would be easy to claim, as pre-Nag 'Hammadi scholars have, that agnostic exegesis of Paul's letters projects a pre- or non-Christian mythological system onto Paul's writings, the Valentinians themselves insist that Paul is their inspiration: they are in the tradition of those who read the Scriptures allegorically or symbolically as they contend Paul intended: '... but he is a Jew, which is one inwardly; and circumcision is that of the heart, in the spirit, and not in the letter...' (*Romans* 2:28f), and as Jesus himself did: '... and without a parable spake he not unto them' (*Matthew* 13:34).

As the great scholar of Gnosticism, Elaine Pagels, says in questioning the way 'conventional exegetical and historical analysis of early Christianity often fails to account for the considerable body of evidence attesting gnostic exegesis of Paul':

'If the apostle were so unequivocally antignostic, how could the gnostics claim him as their great pneumatic [spiritual] teacher? How could they claim his writings as the source for their anthropology, their Christology, and their sacramental theology? How could they say they are following his example when they offer secret teaching of wisdom and gnosis "to the initiates"? How could they claim his resurrection theology as the source of their own, citing his words as decisive evidence *against* the ecclesiastical doctrine of bodily resurrection?'[5]

What St Paul Really Believed

One example from Paul will suffice: 1 *Corinthians* 15, in the New Testament, is the earliest recorded account of Jesus' resurrection. It was probably written in the spring of AD 57. It is a curious chapter, at almost complete odds with the Gospel stories which were written between about 70 and 100 AD.

In fact, the account predates Paul having been 'passed on' to him (v. 3), the original probably dating to the early 30s, not long after Jesus' death.

The Greek of the text is almost certainly a translation and contains a number of Aramaisms and non-Pauline language. In the chapter, Paul lists all the post-resurrection appearances known to him. It is interesting that he goes on to say: 'And if Christ be not risen, then is our preaching vain, and your faith is also vain' (v. 14). The veracity of the Christian faith, for Paul, rests on the 'historical' reality of the resurrection. And nothing more is adduced to support the resurrection than a list of witnesses: Kephas (the Aramaic for Peter), v.5; 'the Twelve', v.5; 'more than 500 of the brothers at the same time', v.6; James, v.7; and lastly, to Paul himself, v.8.

Interestingly, apart from the 'appearance' to Peter, not one of these 'appearances' is to be found in the Gospels, or indeed, elsewhere in the New Testament. Indeed, the truth of the resurrection in the Gospels is adduced from the story of the empty tomb. In all of St Paul's writing he does not once mention the empty tomb.

Paul adds his own name to the list of appearances; this is a reference to his own experience on the road to Damascus recounted in curiously incompatible tales in the book of the *Acts of the Apostles* (9:1-9; 22:5-11; 26:12-18).

In these tales, Jesus' appearance to Paul is in a 'vision' (26:19) from the sky (26:13) and Paul does not differentiate his own vision of the risen Jesus from that of the other appearances he lists.

In 1 *Corinthians* 15, Paul uses the Greek word *egeiro* for 'resurrection'. It generally means 'waking up' or 'rising' (from sleep); it is also, interestingly, the same verb that is used to refer to Jesus' 'ascension' into heaven.

A more interesting word is the one that Paul uses for 'appeared to' (the witnesses): *horao*. There are lots of other everyday words for 'seeing' or 'appearing' in Greek but *horao* is not one of them. The particular form of the verb in 1 *Corinthians,* and elsewhere (*opthe*: third person middle deponent (passive) aorist with the dative), means 'to have a vision'; it is a standard part of the language of revelation.

Paul believed that all post-resurrection appearances of which he knew were in fact, heavenly visions occurring over a period of years. The 'risen' Jesus was in fact the ascended Jesus, appearing in visions from heaven.

In true gnostic fashion, St Paul did not believe in a bodily resurrection of Jesus. That is why he never mentions the empty tomb: he had never heard of such a thing.

Of course, this places Paul at odds with the orthodox tradition of a bodily resurrection, as represented by the Gospels. From the Gospels to Paul, we see the change from an eschatological into a soteriological characterization. More often than not, Christians read Paul's writing on the resurrection through the lens of the corporealized picture painted in the Gospels.

If Paul believes that the resurrection of Jesus is, in fact, a heavenly vision, how far is that defeasible, subject to the scrutiny of historians? More particularly, it may be that in digging the historian's furrow, we misrepresent fundamental early Christian intentions. Dibelius says:

'For Paul, the earthly life of Jesus was not the locus of revelation, but the sphere where the soteriologically necessary humiliation of God's Son took place. Hence Paul needed only to know about the life of Jesus, that it took place, and that Jesus in that life was obedient even unto the Cross. What lies between the Incarnation and the Crucifixion is overcast, but the Gospels tell how this very earthly life was lit up ever and again by heavenly glory which in speech and work broke through every concealment. The variance between the two standpoints was not overcome. Rather this variance provided the theme of the Church's doctrinal disputes on Christology. This variance is found to the present day in the fact that the traditions which the Gospels reproduce from the life of Jesus as signs of revelation are entirely unmentioned in the Creed, because they are not regarded as soteriological facts.'[6]

Notes:

1. Much of the following story can be found in Elaine Pagel's *The Gnostic Gospels*, Penguin, 1982, p. 13ff.
2. p. 295, *A History of the Early Church*, Vol. 1, Lutterworth, 1967.
3. p. 71, *Seven Types of Atheism*, Allen Lane, 2018.
4. See Elaine Pagels, p. 3, *The Gnostic Paul*, Trinity Press International, 1992.
5. *op. cit.* p. 10.
6. *op.* cit. p. 299.

4
Jesus' Teaching

St Paul, along with the Church Fathers, invented Christianity. Whether this faith arose from the life of a failed eschatologist or a deluded revolutionary is of little importance. Ironically, Jesus' teaching plays a very small part in the corpus of theology that goes to make up Christianity.

But even with Jesus' teaching, historical ruminations to establish the defeasibility of that history are not straightforward, particularly when it comes to *recovering* the teaching of Jesus.

Vox Pop

Jesus' message was simple: The Kingdom of Heaven is at hand. Repent and prepare.

Perversely, it might seem, it is the least palatable words of Jesus that are reported in the Gospels that are the most likely to be authentic. Writing two or three generations before the evangelists, St Paul has little interest in what Jesus has to say. But, in the later church, Jesus' sayings became treasured, even when they were difficult to stomach:

He that loveth father or mother more than me is not worthy of me:
And he that loveth son or daughter more than me is not worthy of me.

And he that taketh not his cross, and followeth after me, is not worthy of me. (*Matthew* 10:37 – 38)

It would not be untypical of some of Matthew's sources if these verses were a brief *midrash*, or commentary, on the Old Testament *Micah* 7:6:

For the son dishonoureth the father,
the daughter riseth up against her mother,
the daughter in law against her mother in law;
a man's enemies are the men of his own house.

The New Testament was written in Greek. Jesus spoke (a Galilean version of) Western Aramaic.

A pleasing exercise, designed to recover the spoken words of Jesus, is to translate the Greek into the most likely Western Aramaic that lay behind it and examine the latter to see what transpires.

Taking the so-called 'hard saying' above, we can argue that the occurrence of formal elements of Aramaic poetry in this, and other dominical sayings in the Gospels, points to Aramaic sources. To approach this more safely one could take the Masoretic text of the Micah passage Matthew is using and look for features the Hebrew shares with the purported Aramaic. And here we find alliteration which runs throughout the text in *b;* also the assonance in *en/el* and *ah/ey.*

The incidence of alliteration, assonance, parallelism, paranomasia, wordplay and other such Aramaic poetic devices found here is sufficient to detect the source and thence to approximate the *ipsissima vox*, the real 'voice' – although not the actual words – of Jesus.

Indeed, looking at Luke's version of this hard saying and comparing it with the Masoretic text may lead us to conclude that there was a common underlying source, in Greek or Aramaic, for these particular verses. The expected correspondence between the Masoretic text in the early Greek version of the Old Testament, the Septuagint, shows that it is not too far-fetched to expect the Greek rendering of an Aramaic proto-text (called Q) would produce similar results. Indeed, Luke's inverted or synthetic parallelism might represent adherence to an Aramaic working over of *Micah* 7:6 and Matthew's individualistic rendering might reflect both his own influence but also that of the Greek rendering of an Aramaic source.

In these verses, *Matthew* shows a Christian at odds with (probably) non-Christian relatives; by the time it gets to *Luke* (12:53), we have a family divided. Either way, it would seem to be clear that *Matthew's* vv. 35 ff are an attenuated explanation of the original messianic pronouncement in v. 34 ('Think not that I am come to bring peace on earth: I came not to send peace, but a sword') and that the secondary, midrashic, development was inspired by the primitive Christian community's experience of what discipleship of Jesus meant in human relationships: the obedience required by Jesus must be complete and those who enter the Kingdom must be willing to surrender all, including family. (The reference to taking up the cross, in v. 38, cannot, of course, come from the lips of Jesus.) And all of this is said in an eschatological context (*Matthew* 10:5 – 42). These expectations are what the primitive church believed Jesus required in the Last Days. So, while he can elsewhere call on his disciples to honour their families (*Matthew* 19:19), it is clear that nothing can stand in the way of the demand of obedience to the Kingdom.

There are, of course, dangers in relying on particular verses, or even individual books, of the Bible to develop doctrine or to recover the essence of the message Jesus taught. And yet, the opposite – attempting to achieve an overall view of either doctrine or history – is fraught with hazards and can result in a curious, and utterly unreliable, amalgam.

But even in such exercises as this we are not a great deal closer to discovering *ipsissima verba Jesu*, the actual words Jesus used. The truth is unrecoverable. Dibelius explains the general development of Christianity as passing: 'from a historical person to his formal worship and finally to the cosmic mythological Christ of Gnosis, and to ecclesiastical Christology'[1].

It is simply not possible to recover *any*

of Jesus' actual words. Although the most likely candidates: mainly single-word Aramaic incantations embedded, mostly, in miracle stories, may approximate something of Jesus' speech in his shamanic activity.

Notes:

    1. p. 288, *op. cit.*

IAN WALKER

5

Orthodoxy and Heresy

The early church engaged in trenchant, philosophical debate over the nature of scriptural interpretation. *Plus ça change.* Although most held some general view of the inspiration of the Scriptures, it was more often over the question of interpretation that they disagreed. There were, of course, many areas of disagreement about how Scripture ought to be interpreted but we can distinguish two major schools of thought, both of which cover a broad spectrum of ideas: the *literalists* and the *allegorists* (a battle which, since the twentieth century, still rages, albeit one-sidedly, in Islam).

The literalists: these were the people who believed that Scripture could, somehow or other, be taken 'at face value'; that there is an obvious and evident meaning of the text or, alternatively, that there is no hidden meaning.

A great literalist – a proto-Richard Dawkins – was Porphyry (c. 230 – c. 305), one of Christianity's early detractors. He attacked the allegorizing tendency in the church when he wrote of those 'who boast that the things said plainly by Moses are riddles, treating them as divine oracles, full of hidden mysteries, and bewitching the mental judgement by their own pretentious obscurity, and so they put forward their own interpretations' (*Against the Christians*, III). The attack did not always come from those outside the church. Clement of Alexandria (c. 150 – c. 215) denounced those who do not accept the scripture at its face value: '...but selecting ambiguous expressions, they wrest them to their own opinions, gathering a few expressions, here and there; not looking to the sense, but making use of the mere diction... they attend to the words alone, while they alter the meanings, neither knowing how they are spoken nor using the quotations they adduce according to their true nature' (*Stromateis*, vii 16). A wonderfully ambiguous passage.

The allegorists: of course, not all those who were non-literalists were allegorists but we may use this title because allegorical interpretation was a device common to many.

Possibly as early as AD 70 there is, in the *Epistle of Barnabas*, a strong allegorizing tendency. The author of *Barnabas* thought that the Jews 'shipwrecked' themselves because they took the Scriptures literally and not 'according to the Spirit'. Indeed, understanding the meaning according to the Spirit became a somewhat elitist activity, requiring such things as knowledge of philosophy. Clement (of Alexandria) tells us that

Origen 'instructed many of the less learned in the common school branches [of philosophy], saying that these would be of no small help to them in the study and understanding of the divine Scriptures' (*Strom.* vi 18). It seems that Origen (c. 185 – 254) accepted a threefold division of meaning in Scripture:

'The right way, therefore... of approaching the Scriptures and gathering their meaning is the following, which is extracted from the documents themselves... One must record the meaning of the sacred writings in a threefold way upon one's soul; so that the simple man may be edified by what we may call the flesh of the Scripture, this name being given to the obvious interpretation; while a man who has made some progress may be edified by its soul, as it were; and the man who is perfect... may be edified by the spiritual law... for just as man consists of body, soul and spirit, so in the same way does the Scripture, which has been prepared by God to be given for man's salvation' (*De Principiis*, iv.2.4).

Origen, however, saw that interpretation according to the soul and the spirit is somehow tied to that of the flesh: 'The careful reader will detect thousands of passages like this (Genesis 1) in the gospels, which will convince him that events which did not take place at all were woven into records of what did happen' (*De Prin.* iv.3.1).

Origen, and other Alexandrians, used the historical life of the 'human' Jesus as a point of departure in their quest for the spiritual truth and meaning of Scripture. But even this presupposition was attacked by those allegorists, *par excellence*, the Gnostics. The Valentinians, for example, dismissed as 'literalism' the Church Fathers' 'historical' view of the Gospels. They claim that even the simplest narratives constitute allegories. In fact, the single common link between the diverse methods and results of gnostic interpretation was the belief that the Christians' basic error was their preoccupation with the historical reality of Jesus. Although some, such as Heracleon, did not deny the historicity of all the events in the Gospels, they denied rather that the events have any importance in themselves – on a literal understanding. In support of this, Gnostics turned to the number of passages where Jesus rebukes his hearers for understanding solely on a literal level (e.g. Nicodemus, *John* 3; the Samaritan woman, *John* 4; and Peter is the worst offender [see Irenaeus, *Adversus Haereses* 3.12.9]). For the Gnostics, 'the literal level of any text, then, including that of the gospels, offers only the outward manifestation of inner meaning; it contains the metaphorical form of the ineffable truth'[1].

It was not only those who reflected upon the text of Scripture who exercised the hermeneutical freedom of people like the Gnostics. The Gospel writers themselves, for example, although they do not say anything explicitly about their own hermeneutical methods do display tendencies which reflect a certain freedom of interpretation. For example, if, as is likely, the author(s) of *John* knew *Mark* then his placing of the Cleansing of the Temple and his de-mythologised eschatology (among many other things) cannot reasonably be accounted for except on the basis of theological motivation being allowed to suppress historical accuracy. That is, we might reasonably assume that *John* exercised some hermeneutical presuppositions in his reconstruction of *Markan* chronology and *Markan* accounts of Jesus' teaching.

Hermeneutics remained embroiled in much the same mode as debated by the Church Fathers until the onset of the Enlightenment and the so-called *Quest for the Historical Jesus*.

Notes:
> 1. pp. 15-16, E. Pagels, *The Johannine Gospel in Gnostic Exegesis*, Abingdon, 1973.

6

The Quest for the Historical Jesus

The New Testament faith intends past events; it is, in short, an historical religion. But these past events it intends are no longer directly available and have been subjected to: sophisticated literary editing; apologetic motifs; the intrusion of ecclesiastical formulae which could not have been contemporary with the story being told; the influence of individual narrative style; and so on. A history of Jesus is unobtainable. As such, the New Testament faith cannot be based on data construed in probabilistic, historical terms. Here we must consider the distinction between the Jesus of history and the Christ of faith already evident in the two schools of scriptural interpretation in the early church, bearing in mind the question whether it is possible to have a Christ of faith without an accessible Jesus of history, and which lies at the root of *The Quest for the Historical Jesus*. The *Quest*, a very Protestant and largely German exercise, began around two centuries ago arising from the Enlightenment, notably with the work of writers like Reimarus (1694-1768) and Strauss (1808-1874).

B.F. Meyer tells us that Reimarus, whose hermeneutical guide was *Vernunft* (reason), saw the gospels as motivated by fraud (one must feel sorry for Reimarus who dutifully trotted off to church on Sundays with his family to sit through a service he believed was based on deception); Strauss, led by *Begriff* (idea), sought to neutralize interpretation; Holtzmann and the liberals, in *Historie* (factual history), tried to locate the history of Jesus and skirt around it, while Schweitzer tried to confront it squarely and consign it to the superseded past[1].

And on it goes: late last century it was Bultmann, the German New Testament scholar, and Macquarrie, the Oxford philosopher, who saw Jesus' life through an existentialist lens, Bultmann believing that virtually nothing about Jesus' life could be known and recovering any such data is, now, immaterial anyway. All of them children of the Enlightenment whose hermeneutical tools were inhibiting and reductionist. But the *Quest* was invigorated and deepened by the linguistic insights in Aramaic of Gustav Dalman, Dibelius' Form Criticism, Redaction Criticism and new light on rabbinic sources shed by Paul Billerbeck. In theology, Karl Barth passionately denied efforts to recover the historical Jesus claiming it was unnecessary anyway. After the First World War, the failure of the *Quest* was seen in Barthian circles as a desirable goal.

The *Quest* was revivified with J.M. Robinson's *A New Quest for the Historical Jesus* in 1959. Acknowledging that the original *Quest* had failed in its objective of securing a history of Jesus, the programme for the *New Quest* was now to recover the continuity between Jesus and the *kerygma*, the preaching, of the early church. Quite how such continuities can be captured in the absence of any historical desiderata from the life of Jesus remains a mystery. And this mystery continues in spite of the writings of Joachim Jeremias, whose work represents the scholarly apotheosis of all *Quest* enquiries: for Jeremias, the early, Easter church preserved the *kerygma* of Jesus' transcending words and deeds; this was all that was needed. In spite of his unrivalled erudition, Jeremias never manages to cross the 'broad, ugly ditch' between the unknowable Jesus of history and the Christ of faith. But we need to consider whether this dichotomy is misleading. Consider Wittgenstein:

'It has been said that Christianity rests on an historic basis.

'It has been said a thousand times by intelligent people that indubitability is not enough in this case. Even if there is as much evidence as for Napoleon. Because the indubitability wouldn't be enough to make me change my whole life.

'It doesn't rest on an historic basis in the sense that ordinary belief in historic facts could serve as a foundation.

'Here we have belief in historic facts different from a belief in ordinary historic facts. Even, they are

not treated as historical, empirical, propositions.
'Those people who had faith didn't apply the doubt which would ordinarily apply to *any* historical propositions. Especially propositions of a time long past, etc.'[2]

For Wittgenstein, faith is not derived from the historicity of the Bible:
'Christianity is not based on a historical truth: rather, it offers us a (historical) narrative and says: now believe. But not: believe this narrative with the belief appropriate to a historical narrative; rather, believe through thick and thin, which you can do only as a result of a life. Here you have a narrative; don't take the same attitude as you take to other historical narratives. Make quite a different place in your life for it.'[3]

The metaphysical fiction of 'factuality' is persistent. As Wittgenstein suggests, talk of 'facts' in religion will be different from talk of facts in other contexts: in the context of God's revelation, what the facts are will take on a new light. But here we encounter the difficulty of how events can, in *any* case, be seen as revelatory, as God communicating with mankind. Indeed, are there *any* facts of history which can be known sufficiently well to evince the commitment of faith? I doubt it. As Anthony Kenny suggests: 'Unless the relevant stories can be as certain as the commitment which faith demands of the believer, the commitment is, so far forth as it is faith, irrational; and if the belief is a commitment which is rationally in proportion to the support given by the history, it is, so far forth as it is rational, something less than faith.'[4]

The newest iteration of the *Quest* has now turned inward, looking away from sources and leaning, having been boosted by Jeremias' undoubted achievements, to investigating historiographical method and philosophy.

Notes:

1. p. 25, *The Aims of Jesus*, SCM, 1979.
2. p. 57, *Lectures and Conversations on Aesthetics, Psychology & Religious Belief*, Blackwell, 1970.
3. p. 32, *Culture and Value*, Blackwell, 1980.
4. p. 83, *Faith and Reason,* CUP, 1983.

7
It Was Not Always So

Not only was the history of Jesus inextricably bound with the confession of the primitive church but propositional belief played no part in the faith of early Christians. The word *belief* originally connoted something entirely different: it had a non-propositional meaning. The Latin word for what we mean by belief today is *opinio*; this is not a biblical, nor indeed a religious, category.

The conspicuous Latin word in religious language is *credo* (literally: 'I set my heart', from *cor, cordis*, heart, and *+-do, +-dere,* to put). The church, from the earliest days and as late as Vatican I (1869 – 1870), construed *credo* – translated as 'I believe' in the first words of the creeds – as a religious category, not as belief, a propositional matter, but as faith, a form of commitment, a setting one's heart.

The Anglo-Saxon 'believe' originally had a meaning closer to that of 'faith' than, say, *opinio*. German: *bei lieben*, to hold dear, to prize, or to love. And Latin: *libido*. Today, we wrongly read a modern propositional connotation into the words of the creed following 'I believe ...'

As late as 1611, it is not possible to find a concept

of belief in the modern sense in the Bible. Ancient meanings are best not construed thus through a modern lens: faith is not belief. Faith is concerned with the personal relationship established by trust. Faith, in its 'intellectual' guise, is insight, recognition; it is a developing vision which leads to commitment. Faith, like courage or loyalty, is a human virtue.

Socrates' paradox tells us that all virtues are one which, if true, removes faith entirely from the realm of propositional belief.

What can be said of faith in the early Christian writers can be said of the authors of the *Bhagavad-Gita*, the *Vedas*, the *Upanishads*, the *Old Testament*, the *Qu'ran,* and even in such rationalising texts as the *Kathavathu Kamma* debates of the *Pali* Canon.

Not only was the *Quest*, inevitably, a failure but much of Scripture is resistant to *Quest*-like endeavours. A few examples of this impossibility, in more general biblical terms, will suffice.

8
The Folly of Belief

Bishop James Ussher (1581 – 1656) was the Church of Ireland Archbishop of Armagh and Primate of All Ireland; he was a prolific scholar who, using the Old Testament, ancient history, astronomy, ancient calendars and chronology wrote *Annales veteris testament a prima mundi origine deducti*, in which he attempted to calculate the date of creation; this he gave as around nightfall on 22nd October, 4004 BC. Sir Isaac Newton, interestingly possibly an Asperger's sufferer, also attempted to resolve this conundrum.

But that particular tree up which they barked was the wrong one: early Judaism was not monotheistic but henotheistic (Greek: one god among the pantheon) devoted to the exclusive worship of Yahweh. Genesis 1:1 – 2:4, the story of creation, is in fact an anti-astral deity polemic written in sixth century BC Babylon. The Jews who wrote it, probably using an earlier pagan document to parody, did not deny the existence of other gods, some of whom are named in the Hebrew text (e.g., *Shemesh/Shamash, Laylah*) of that first chapter of the Bible. But the Jews' God, named variously *Yahweh* or *El* or *Elohim* (interestingly plural) is the one, true God of them all.

Ussher and his modern-day counterparts – and there are surprisingly many of them – miss the point: *Genesis* is a part-polemic, part-aetiological myth – a story told to explain some current feature of the natural or social world; these are not history subject to verification, nor were they intended to be by those who wrote them. One can only tell the story in the hope that it will enlighten one's quest for meaning. But what is truly surprising is that the later Victorian and current wrangle between science and religion persists. I suppose that as long as there are evangelical atheists and theists who misunderstand, and insist on misinterpreting the nature of faith as propositional belief, we will be beset by such tedious nonsenses.

Many of the early *Genesis* stories are aetiological (told within the overall context of answering the question: how did the world come about?). For example: why are there two sexes propagated by sexual intercourse? Because (in shades reminiscent of Plato's *Symposium*): '... and the rib, which the Lord God had taken from man, made he a woman, and brought her unto the man. And Adam said, This is now bone of my bones, and flesh of my flesh: she shall be called Woman [Hebrew: *ishshah* but later called Eve = *havah* = 'life' by Adam], because she was taken out of Man [Hebrew: *adam* = man]. Therefore shall a man leave his father and mother, and shall cleave unto his wife: and they shall become one flesh' (*Gen.* 2: 22-24). Why are snakes without legs? Because, having beguiled the woman to eat the forbidden fruit: '... the Lord God said unto the serpent, Because thou hast done this, thou art cursed above all cattle... upon thy belly thou shalt go, and dust shalt thou eat all the days of thy life...' (*Gen.* 3: 14). Why do women have pain in childbirth? Because, following Eve's disobedience: 'Unto the woman he said, I will greatly multiply thy sorrow and thy conception; in sorrow thou shalt bring forth children... '(*Gen.* 3:16). Why do people speak different languages? Because, even though originally 'the whole earth was of one language', following men's vanity in attempting to build a tower (of Babel) 'whose top may reach unto heaven', to punish their arrogance God decided to: '... confound their language, that they may not understand one another's speech' (*Gen.* 11: 7). And so on...

Interestingly, Australian aboriginal (Neolithic) religion – tales from the *Dreamtime* - is nothing *but* aetiological. For example: how did Uluru (Ayer's Rock) come about? It was built as a corroboree ground (a ground prepared for ritual song and dance) by Kunapipi, the serpent goddess. Why do dogs bark? Because, following their noisome disobedience at the corroboree, Kunapipi withdrew their powers of speech as a punishment. And so on...

Thus the real challenge comes to those religions

which intend, and are in some degree based on, historical events. In this sense, the failure of *The Quest for the Historical Jesus* could prove fatal to a faith based on the life, death and resurrection of Jesus (the same might be said *mutatis mutandis* for Abraham and Mohammed), but, as we have seen with St Paul, even such ruminations as these may miss the mark. It is impossible to extract fact from fiction in the histories of these men.

Some further examples might help.

Noah

Noah's flood (*Genesis* 6:5 – 9:17) is taken from the *Gilgamesh Epic*, a much earlier, traditional Mesopotamian tale of The Deluge, a great flood whereby in the early days of human history the gods sought mankind's destruction. In the *Atram-hasis* poem from the Old Babylonian period, we have the history of mankind from the creation to the flood during which Atram-hasis builds his curious ark to escape the deluge. He survives, with his family, his riches and representatives of each craft and species of animal. The ark is grounded on a high mountain peak where Atram-hasis offers thanks to the gods for his survival. After the deluge, man's lifespan is to be set: death is naturally now to follow life: '... And all the days of Noah were 950 years: and he died' (*Genesis* 9:29).

The *Atram-hasis* poem is later used by the poet of *Gilgamesh*, thus providing a striking model for

Noah's story.

The Sojourn in Egypt

The Old Testament is clear that the early tribes of Israel spent over 400 years in Egypt until their liberation by Moses who led them to the Promised Land (*Exodus* 12:40). The Exodus story is vivid and the Egyptians were excellent record-keepers. But there is no extra-biblical evidence of Joseph's arrival in Egypt with his technicolour dream-coat (actually, in Hebrew: a long, sleeved robe), of the tribes as slaves or of their departure from Egypt under Moses' leadership. Indeed, there is good reason to doubt it.

Despite extensive contemporary records, not one reference is to be found of the presence of the Tribes of Israel in Egypt: no Joseph – supposedly Pharaoh's Chancellor. Egyptian elements and motifs in the Joseph story place it firmly in the seventh century BC at the earliest, far too late to reflect the tale of the Patriarchs and the tribal bondage in Egypt. Like so much of the book of *Genesis*, it is aetiological, used to explain the cause of the tribes' trek to Palestine. There is no Moses, no exodus, entailing a pharaoh's death.

Or was the story of Moses leading an exodus a reworking on a grand scale of the earlier tale in *Genesis* 12 where Abraham avoids famine in Palestine by escaping to Egypt, passes Sarah his wife off as his sister who is then adopted into

Pharaoh's harem, a consequence of which means riches for Abraham? Eventually, God visits plagues on the Pharaoh for his sins and Abraham and Sarah are expelled.

In literary terms, it is highly likely that these stories are folktale motifs belonging to the 'Patriarchs'; it features three times in *Genesis*: Abraham does the same trick with Abimelech 'King of the Gerar' (*Genesis* 20). His son Isaac tries it on with another Abimelech, anachronistically 'King of the Philistines', with his wife Rebecca (*Genesis* 26).

Moses

Moses being pulled from the water by Pharaoh's daughter (*Exodus* 2:1 – 10) is, in fact, an Akkadian tale from a thousand years earlier. The Akkadian Empire at its height stretched from the Gulf to Levantine Syria and was built by Sargon the Great and his successors. The legend tells how Sargon was found:

My mother, a priestess, conceived me and bore me in secret,
She put me in the basket of reeds, sealed its lid with pitch;
She cast me adrift on the river from which I could not arise,
The river bore me up and brought me to Aqqi, a drawer of water.
He took me as his son and reared me.

Indeed, the name Moses itself is something of a giveaway. In Middle Egyptian, as in many Ancient Near Eastern and sub-Egyptian languages, vowels were pronounced but not written. 'Moses', written SSM (Hebrew is read from right to left) is thought to mean 'drawer out' (cf. Aqqi) and, with different vowels, could easily be read as MaSeS but also MoSeS or MoSiS (the Bohairic form). His name suggests royal birth, a suitable Egyptian name for a borrowed myth. In fact, however, SSM simply means 'son of', as in Son of Ra (Ramases) or Son of Thoth (Tuthmosis).

There is no extra-biblical evidence for the existence of Moses. If, as seems likely, the bondage in Egypt was written in the seventh or sixth century BC when a Babylonian threat of invasion of Palestine loomed large, then the affirmation of an earlier bondage from which there was a divine delivery can be seen as a statement of hope and faith, not a record of history.

It is unlikely that the Patriarchs, the fathers of the Israelites, Abraham, Isaac and Jacob, existed but these myths illumine the meaning of many people's lives. But Israel, according to Old Testament tradition, was an association of twelve separate tribes and cannot, according to Noth, 'be grasped as a historical entity until it becomes a reality living on the soil of Palestine'[1], doubtless in the Bronze Age and doubtless not all arriving at the same time. The fundamental constituent of the Patriarch tradition lies in the divine promises to 'Israel' in occupying and possessing the land of Palestine; promises which are still claimed today.

The tradition of the Patriarchs grew once the Tribes were settled and served to codify their rights to the appropriated land. Local Palestinian traditions became attached to the now-named figures of the Patriarchs. It is likely that the stories of the Patriarchs in early Judaism under the amphictyonic confederacy of the Twelve Tribes were locally acquired, secondary traditions: the whole story of Sodom (*Genesis* 18 to 19); the aetiology of the substitution of the sacrifice of a son by that of a ram in the mountain sanctuary in 'the land of Moriah' (*Genesis* 22:1 – 19); the story of the Negeb wells of both Abraham and Isaac (*Genesis* 21.25 f; 30; 26:14 f); the story of Jacob and Esau which are native to the land of Gilead including the aetiology of the Israelite – Aramaean frontier on 'mount Gilead' (*Genesis* 31) and the story of the night-spirit at the Jabbok ford near Peniel (*Genesis* 32:23 – 32), and many others.

The recovery of the history of the Patriarchs is impossible: the Bible stories represent a cross-cultural matrix of myth and legend. This history is irrecoverably buried in myths and is no longer accessible to us. All we can do is tell the stories.

And what of the nomological nature of *Leviticus*

and *Deuteronomy*? Or the poetry of the *Psalms*? Or the pithy apophthegms of *Proverbs*? Or the seductive imagery of the *Song of Songs*? Or the jeremiads of the Prophets? Or the epistolatory tone of Paul's letters? Or even the apocalyptical hocus pocus of the book of *Revelation*? What is the propositional knife-wielder to make of these? It is a mistake to assume that religious literature and belief constitutes, or is even of the same order as, inferences from observations of the world to the divine reality.

Notes:

    1. p. 53, *The History of Israel,* A & C Black, 1960.

9
The Value of Myth

Almighty God, our heavenly Father, guide, we beseech thee, the nations of the world into the ways of justice and truth. Establish among them that peace which is the fruit of righteousness; and grant that in every land thy kingdom may come and thy will be done; through Jesus Christ our Lord.
American Prayer Book

There is nothing intrinsically wrong with most religions; it is man who is fundamentally flawed – a lesson religion has taught for millennia. Christian belief is not wrong; it is simply naïve. And the secular faiths based on it are equally naïve: hopes of human progress, as seen in the prayer above, are doomed to fail. But that such hopes persist should not surprise us. Humans have an extraordinary capacity for self-delusion. An interesting question is why this should be so: it may have to do with the fact that deception – whether of self or others – is a more efficacious Darwinian device than honesty.

While the doctrine of *heilsgeschichte* – history teleologically directed to salvation for all believers – is a utopian myth, the doctrine of original sin – that man is fundamentally and irrevocably flawed – is a great insight. But how these doctrines can be simultaneously held is a mystery. The hope of salvation for all will never be realised precisely because of the truth that all men are sinners. But to tether us to the eschatological hope of salvation is a harmful myth when, in reality, we should be learning to live in perpetual conflict, the natural outcome of the human condition.

The Virgin Birth

The doctrine of the Virgin Birth is based on a piece of linguistic chicanery. Or, dare I say, rests on a misconception.

The birth narratives (in *Matthew* and *Luke* only) tell us: 'Now all this was done, that it might be fulfilled which was spoken of the Lord by the prophet, saying, Behold, a virgin shall be with child, and shall bring forth a son, and they shall call his name Emmanuel...' (*Matthew* 1: 22-23) and the prophet being quoted is (first) *Isaiah* 7: 14: 'Therefore the Lord himself shall give you a sign; Behold, a virgin shall conceive, and bear a son, and shall call his name Immanuel.'

In first Isaiah, the Hebrew word used for what is translated as 'virgin' is *ha-almah* which means 'young woman', either married or unmarried. It does not mean 'virgin'. The Hebrew word for 'virgin' is *bethulah*.

In *Matthew* and *Luke*, the Greek word used to translate *ha-almah* is *parthenos* which *does* mean 'virgin'. The word we would naturally expect to render 'young woman' (*ha-almah*) into Greek is *gune* (= woman) but they have chosen instead *parthenos*. Thus, a purposeful mistranslation of the Old Testament word *ha-almah* has led to a virgin birth.

Doubtless this can be accounted for by the fact that it was often assumed of great men at the time, since Homer and including Plato and Alexander the Great, that they had been born of a god. But *ha-almah* does not mean virgin – for which *bethulah* is a perfectly good Hebrew word – and *parthenos* is not a proper translation of it. By the time of King James I (1611), the doctrine had become so entrenched that even James' translators of the 'Authorised Version' saw the Hebrew word through the lens of the Greek *parthenos* (rather than the other way around) that they happily mistranslated *ha-almah* as 'virgin'.

Euripides, the fifth century BC Greek playwright, wrote a play called *Ion*. Ion eventually becomes King of Athens and patriarch of the Ionian race. It is remarkable just how similar many aspects of the play are to various features of the life of Jesus: Ion is the son of a god whose mother is particularly vague about how he came to be born but, in spite of this, he struggles with his own semi-divine identity. He is persecuted by a rabble but in the end takes his just and honourable possession.

The birth narratives of Jesus in the Gospels are pure myth. I don't mean to suggest the silly thesis that there is, in some way or other, an historical connection between the birth narratives in the Gospels and Euripides' play. What I find interesting, however, is that for Euripides the important questions are the ones that are entirely absent from those in the Gospels and they reflect on Ion's integrity and intelligence, coalescing, as they do, in his search for the truth.

By the time of Euripides, it was for educated Athenians – he lived in Athens – no longer a question of believing or disbelieving in myths or miracles: that question the Athenian intellect could settle for itself. But the uneasiness of superstition survives the victory of the intellect. In the end, Ion decides that it will be either Apollo or the truth, and if they do not tally, it will be the truth. Such a consideration, informatively, does not arise in the Gospels. On the other hand, myth as a vehicle of insight and truth must not be underestimated whether in Euripides *or* the Gospels. Myth-making is part of the fabric of what it is to be human.

Here we might consider the work of Teilhard de Chardin (1881 – 1955) which represents perhaps the apotheosis – or is it the nadir? - of Christian myth dressed up as science. De Chardin was a Jesuit priest and an eminent scientist specialising in evolution. In *The Phenomenon of Man*, de Chardin, building from his observation of simple elements, identified complex unities: particles into atoms, atoms into molecules, molecules into living cells, cells into multicellular organisms. He then makes the jump that from this increasing complexity of life goes a corresponding increase in the direction of life and consciousness; this evolutionary advance can be witnessed not only on earth but universally and the key to its development here on earth is the advent of reflective thought in man; this event he calls 'hominization'. The appearance of humans adds a new layer to the physical layers that go to make up the earth's surface, the 'biosphere', but also the new (thinking) layers of man and his creations, the 'noosphere'. Leaving science in a darkened corner of the laboratory, de Chardin then extrapolates this revolutionary process into the future: consciousness and complexity will continue to evolve until they reach the 'omega-point', a suprapersonal unity of all things in God. Thus God is the final, rather than the efficient, cause of the universe, drawing all things towards perfection in Himself.

This is neither faith nor science; it is myth, pure and simple. But it is a damaging myth suggesting as it does the gradual perfectibility of both humans and the planet whereas the truth lies in precisely the opposite direction: humankind by its nature cannot move inexorably to perfection and all things tend to entropy.

Unlike the enlightening and beautiful aetiological myth of Adam and Eve in Eden, de Chardin's myth is ugly and misleading: a fusion of pseudoscience and salvation-history offering no insight or beauty.

In the end, when it comes to miracles and myth, all you can do is tell the story. As the Emperor Julian said of mythology: 'These things never happened, and yet they are eternally true.'

10

Propositional Belief and the Problem of Evidence

I have, hitherto, spoken of evidence adduced in support of propositional belief as if it were uniform and unproblematical. This is not so. Richard Swinburne (1934- present) is Emeritus Professor of Philosophy at the University of Oxford and an influential proponent of arguments for the existence of God. Swinburne is a Christian apologist and a successor of Hume. I shall use one of Swinburne's arguments to show that not only does his argument, and, *mutatis mutandis,* other arguments like it, fail but that the notions of evidence he employs (which are not untypical) are inadequate.

Swinburne argues that religious belief is: largely propositional; supported by evidence (from the total evidence available) and that an increase in probability is sufficient for evidence. I shall show he is wrong. Swinburne employs *Baye's Theorem* (formulated by the Rev. Thomas Bayes (1702-1761) – the theorem is widely used, particularly in assessing drug testing and cancer rates):

Someone who evaluates an hypothesis (H) on the basis of evidence (E) brings to its assessment:

i)   a prior degree of confidence in H;

ii)   prior expectations whether E should occur if H is correct; and

iii)   a prior degree of confidence that E should (or should not) occur regardless of whether H is true [1]

and, *The Principle of Reasonable Belief* which holds that:

If, in the light of background information B, E is evidence that H, then, given B, E is at least good reason for believing H.

As I address the question of miracles below, it will be apposite to consider Swinburne's Argument from Miracles[2]. It is helpful for our purposes that Swinburne speaks here of the resurrection:

'Among the major theistic religions more has been claimed for one such phenomenon than for any others – and that phenomenon is of course the life, death, and resurrection of Jesus of Nazareth… For many Christians these remarkable events have been evidence not merely that the God in whom they already believed was at work in a particular way, telling men a particular message, but evidence that there is a God.'

Our brief consideration of the New Testament gives rise to a challenge to Swinburne's statement: certainly, the events were construed by the early church as evidence that 'the God in whom they already believed was at work in a particular way', but we did not encounter any indication that the resurrection, nor any other event, was construed by them as 'evidence that there is a God'. But let us for the moment overlook this problem. Swinburne also correctly notes that whether or not such purported events occurred is crucial: 'so we need, as well as arguments to show that if the events occurred God brought them about, arguments to show that they did occur.'

Briefly, Swinburne's argument runs like this: when is some particular historical event such that it is very improbable that it would occur through natural processes? It is not probable that natural processes will bring about E if our evidence makes it probable that physical objects do not have the power to bring about E. Natural laws codify generalisations about the powers of physical objects (Swinburne covers laws construed both as universal and as statistical generalisations). It is not probable that natural processes will bring about an event E if the occurrence of E is incompatible with the universal operation of the laws of nature. Violations are clearly not explicable by natural processes and natural laws lead us to assume they will not occur. So: 'where K records that the world is governed by fairly deterministic natural laws and E records the occurrence of a violation... And H is the hypothesis of theism, P (E/– H.K) [the probability of E, given not H and K] will be low. For if there is no power beyond natural laws to determine what happens, one would expect what happens to accord with natural laws.' Yet, 'if natural laws operate because God makes them operate, then since God is equally able to make events occasionally occur not in occurrence with natural laws, the occurrence of the occasional violation... is much more to be expected. For then there is in being a power easily able to bring about such events; but otherwise all the powers in being are such as militate against the occurrence of such events[3] ... Hence the occurrence of violations... would confirm the existence of God'.

Swinburne then ties this argument to a further one: 'From the Character of God'[4] which has to do with the question of whether there are events such that God would have reason to bring them about. In other words, E may be such that its occurrence is more to be expected if there is a God than if there is not. So, 'If P(E/H.K) exceeds P(E/K) [the probability of E given H and K exceeds the probability of E given K] because God has reason... to bring E about rather than some events which would otherwise be equally likely with E to occur, then the occurrence of E confirms the existence of God.' God does have some such good reasons, some of which Swinburne suggests (e.g., to correct failure of growth in moral and religious knowledge, the alleviation of suffering, etc.); therefore, some such events confirm the existence of God.

What are we to make of Swinburne's argument here? My first concern has to do with the concept of evidence he employs. The notion of evidence may mean different things in different contexts; it has, as do words generally, a range of meaning. Generally speaking, when evidence is brought into play it suggests that the matter for which x is evidence is not certain. If I say 'the grass is green', I am usually expressing something I take for granted; something about which I have no doubts. I do not need to mention my certainty. But if I say 'I am sure (or certain) that the grass is green', then I show that the matter may be open to dispute (even if I don't happen to believe anything other than that the grass is green). If I support my statement by the production of evidence then I'm usually showing that my statement is vulnerable to criticism, even though I believe it will stand up to a challenge. If I say that there is evidence that an intruder has entered my house, that it's not simply in a different state of order from the time I last left it because of the wind blowing the papers off the table, etc., I then go on to show my interlocutor why this is so. I show her the slight rearrangement of papers inside my desk, how the curtains are now wide open when I was convinced I had only left them half open, and so on. I'm not saying that I am sure someone has been in my room in the way that I might be if I had seen him enter myself and had taken a photograph to corroborate my statement.

Evidence for beliefs vary and our grounds for believing them are not equally strong or weak. But those matters which we claim to know are not in this way subject to modification (unless, that is, we find ourselves in the not unusual situation where we say that we thought we knew but were shown by the relevant evidence not to have known but to have been mistaken).

If I say 'I know I have german measles, these lumps and rash are evidence', and it transpires that it was not german measles but simply a reaction induced by contact with a poisonous plant, it may then be correct to say: 'I did not know I had german measles, I was mistaken.' But is it also correct to say that the lumps and the rash were not evidence for german measles, even though they corresponded with the symptoms associated with people suffering from german measles? It may be safe to say that the lumps and rash might have been evidence of german measles but, as it transpired, they were not. In other words, they were evidence of something, but not of german measles. That is, we argue that these features were never evidence of german measles. Or do we argue that they were evidence of german measles but are not now? Or do we argue that they were evidence of german measles and that they still are (even though it transpires that I do not have german measles)? Each of these possible responses indicates something of the various features which may, among others, be associated with the use of evidence and which, depending on the way they are used, lead to confusion.

It might be better, rather than arguing that only one of these responses is correct in this instance, to consider the possibility that they all represent different uses of evidence which, in different contexts, are entirely appropriate. In the last instance, viz. that the lumps and rash were and still are evidence, we can imagine circumstances where this is reasonable and we may also identify certain characteristics of such instances. Suppose, for example, that 57% of a certain electorate said that they would vote Conservative in the next election. This is evidence that roughly 57% of those voting would vote Conservative, given that the sample was well-conducted and that such samples are usually accurate. We might call this type of evidence *possible evidence*. From our example we could note that its main feature is that E can be possible evidence for H even if H is false. Furthermore, E is possible evidence for H independently of anyone's beliefs about E or H or their relationship to one another (this is what Carnap calls 'the classificatory concept of confirmation').

The first notion of evidence, viz. that the lumps and rash are not and never were evidence of german measles, may be called the notion of *actual evidence*. It runs to the effect that E is actual evidence that H only if E is possible evidence that H and H is true.

The second notion of evidence, viz. that the lumps/rash were evidence but are not now, may be called the *subjective* notion of evidence. This concept turns on the feature of someone's possessing the evidence. Previously my evidence that I had german measles was that I had lumps and a rash. This involves the claim that previously I believed that the lumps and rash were possible evidence of german measles. However, this is no longer sufficient if now my lumps/rash are possible evidence of german measles, for the fact that I have lumps and a rash is not now my evidence that I have german measles, even if I now believe that it is possible evidence. We would therefore have to strengthen the claim to read that the fact that I have lumps and a rash is actual evidence of german measles.

When we say that my lumps/rash were, but no longer are, evidence of german measles we are referring to someone's evidence; in this case, mine. This notion of evidence is quite subjective: whether E is my evidence that H depends entirely on what I believe about E, about H, and their relationship, and whether in fact E is possible or actual evidence that H.

It is often argued that evidence bears some relationship to what it is reasonable to believe. This is sometimes formulated, as we have seen above, as the Principle of Reasonable Belief (PRB):

If, in the light of background information B, E is evidence that H, then, given B, E is at least some good reason for believing H.

This principle is satisfied by the conditions of our first and last notions of evidence, i.e., possible and actual evidence, which may both be seen under the heading of *objective* evidence. If, in the light of the background information B that lumps and a certain rash are generally associated with german measles, the fact that I have these symptoms is possible or actual evidence that I have german measles, then, given B, the fact that I do have lumps and a certain rash is at least some good reason for believing that I have german measles.

The subjective notion, however, does not satisfy the PRB. The fact that I live in Oxfordshire where good cricketers are born may be my evidence that my wife is going to bear a baby boy. But this is not a good reason at all, even for me, to believe this hypothesis.

Possible Evidence and Probability

Swinburne offers a definition of possible evidence in terms of probability whereby:

'E is possible evidence that H iff [if and only if] the probability of H given E is greater than the prior probability of H. So, i) E is possible evidence that H if P(H/E) > P(H) [the probability of H given E is greater than the probability of H]. Or, if B is background information, ii) E is possible evidence that H iff P(H/E.B) > P(H/B) [the probability of H given E and B is greater than the probability of H given B].'

However, if 'evidence' and 'probability' are used as they are in everyday language and in science, there are discrepancies in this definition. First, neither of Swinburne's conditions requires that E be true. As we have seen, this seems to be necessary for evidence. That I have lumps and a rash is not evidence that I have german measles if I do not have lumps and a rash! But even the inclusion of a truth-requirement will not make for a satisfactory definition. I shall offer two examples: the first is designed to show that an increase in probability is not sufficient for evidence, and the second to show that it is not necessary.

The Numbers Out of a Hat Case[5]

Let B be the background information that on Saturday 1000 tickets, numbered 1 – 1000 will be placed in a hat and that one ticket will be drawn out. Let E be the information that on Friday night tickets numbered 101 – 1000 are withdrawn and destroyed. Let H be the hypothesis that the number 50 will be drawn out of the hat. On Thursday, the probability that the number 50 would be drawn out of the hat was 1 in 1000, but on Saturday morning, the probability that 50 will be drawn out of the hat has been increased tenfold and is now 1 in 100. Although there has been an increase in the probability of H, it is surely not evidence that the number 50 will be drawn out of the hat. If anything is likely to happen, we would expect that any of the numbers 1 – 49 and 51 – 100 will be drawn.

According to Swinburne's PRB, if E is possible evidence that the number 50 will be drawn out of the hat then, given B, E is at least some good reason for believing that H. But the reverse seems to be the case. In the light of B, E is not a good reason for believing that H at all. So, in this instance at least, the increase in probability is not sufficient for evidence.

There are countless occurrences which increase the probability of certain consequences. But the fact that such events occur is not necessarily evidence for expecting such consequences. If I stand under an apple tree, I increase the probability that I will be hit on the head by a falling apple; but the fact that I'm standing under an apple tree is not evidence that I will be hit on the head by a falling apple. When someone eats food, she increases the probability that she will contract food poisoning; but the fact that she is now eating an ice lolly is not evidence that she will contract food poisoning.

These examples show that for E to be evidence that H it is not sufficient that E increases H's probability. The next example is does designed to show that it's not even necessary.

The Paradox of Ideal Evidence

Let B be the background information that in the first 1000 flips of cards at random from this pack of 52, the cards, shuffled after each flip, came up on cards other than the nine of hearts approximately 51/52nds of the time. Let E be the information that in the second thousand flips of the cards, shuffled in like manner, the cards came up on numbers other than the nine of hearts approximately 51/52nds of the time.

Let H be the hypothesis that on the 2001st flip of the cards, the card turned up will be other than the nine of hearts. This would seem reasonable: P (H/ E.B) = (H/B) = 51/52.

In other words, E does not change the probability that H which in turn means that E is not evidence that H (according to Swinburne's (ii) above). But this claim does seem unreasonable. Even though there is other evidence that H (B), the fact of E is relevant to H and indeed is evidence for it. That is, E can be evidence that H even if there is other equally good evidence that H. The first 1000 flips may be adequate evidence that H but this does not mean that the second thousand flips is not.

I suggest therefore that 'E is evidence that H' cannot simply be defined in terms of 'E increases H's probability'.

Some writers, including Swinburne, try to avoid this difficulty by a revision of the definition of evidence in terms of probability; in this case where the definition is maintained but seen to be greater than K where K is some number, say one half. While this revision accommodates my two examples it still encounters problems. The first question is the relevance of K for E. It is, for example, irrelevant to the hypothesis H that the earth is round that E, Boris Johnson prefers to wear blue ties. The probability of H is very high, and is not diminished by the assumption of E, but E is not evidence that H. Swinburne could counter such a criticism by incorporating his background information (which in this case is K, that the earth is round) into the probability statement itself. But the introduction of irrelevant information still causes problems.

At this point we can consider Swinburne's 'Argument from the Character of God', which appeals to the notion of explanation or reasonable explanation:

a) a miracle M is observed;
b) M would be more expected (or better explained)

if H (there is a God) is true;
c) therefore, this is some reason to believe that H.

The observance of M is possible evidence that H. But the fact, if it is a fact, that Jesus rose from the dead (M) may be possible evidence that H (there is a God) even though H does not, and would not if true, best explain why Jesus rose from the dead. The most expected, or best explained condition, if necessary, should require only some explanatory connection between H and M. But neither will this thesis provide sufficient conditions: suppose that I wake this morning to find that I have a roaring toothache (E). The hypothesis that last night I received a knock on the mouth when I ran into the bedroom door knob in a drunken state having consumed two bottles of whisky (H) would, if true, explain why I do have a roaring toothache this morning. Even if H is true, the fact that E is true is not evidence that H is true because it is not the case that H is probable given E. Is the fact, for example, that I have certain lumps and a rash possible evidence that I have german measles? The fact that I have certain lumps and a rash is possible evidence that I have german measles only if it is probable that I have german measles, given that I do have certain lumps and a rash, and that it is probable that there is some explanatory connection between the two. Whether such probability conditions apply depends on what background information is being assumed.

Furthermore, Swinburne's argument could be said to violate the PRB, whereby, if E is evidence that H, then this would constitute some good reason for my believing that H. But given what would usually constitute relevant background information for such a case as my toothache, the fact that I have a toothache this morning is a very slim reason for believing the specific type of hypothesis H. Many other hypotheses could be offered which would correctly explain why I have a toothache:

H1 – I have not been to the dentist for the last twenty years.
H2 – I have had a toothache in that spot (and many others) in my mouth (every second morning, only on Thursdays, etc.) for the last twenty years.
H3 – I've not cleaned my teeth in twenty years and only have one tooth left in my head, and that one is rotting and decaying, etc.

Is the fact that I have a toothache this morning evidence that H1 ($- 3^n$) is true, and is it reasonable for me to believe any such hypotheses?

We are now in a better position to assess Swinburne's arguments and to consider how they meet the criteria necessary for such an argument to work. First then, as we have seen, E is possible evidence that H only if E is true. Is it true that, in relation to the event we have been considering, the resurrection, that E is true? Our examination of the data showed that not only is the evidence insufficient to offer sound historical proof for the resurrection but it is subject to not a little doubt that the resurrection, in the view of the biblical writers, constitutes a violation of the kind Swinburne identifies as supporting his argument. Here it is important to note that it is not just 'ordinary' events that Swinburne wants to use in his argument:

'I have in mind particularly striking miracles, generally believed to have occurred by the inhabitants of some small spatio-temporal region of the earth – sudden recoveries from cancer leaving no trace; and growing a new limb from the stump of an amputated limb, or perhaps a striking and sudden recovery of sanity – these events occurring in the context of a religious tradition of prayer for them to happen.'

Here Swinburne appears to be mirroring examples adduced by Hume.

So for E to be possible evidence that H, E must be true. Given that we cannot show that E is true, at least in the way Swinburne requires it to be true (as a violation miracle), then we cannot show that it is possible evidence that H. I have shown that we cannot show that E is true in this sense, so E is not possible evidence that H.

Secondly, for E to be possible evidence that H it is necessary that E does not entail H. In other words, it is necessary that 'Jesus rose from the dead' does not entail that 'God exists'. In my consideration of miracles and violations below I shall show that, although the two statements E and H do not mutually entail one another, given the sense which violation miracles requires then E in fact, given its setting in the religious context, does entail H. The second condition for this argument to work is, therefore, violated. Furthermore, as a matter of historical fact, the early church did not assert H in the way that Swinburne wants to. They said 'God raised Jesus from the dead' and 'Jesus was raised from the dead' (passive, with the implication that God did it), but they did not say something like: 'God exists, and the evidence for this is that he raised Jesus from the dead', or 'the fact that Jesus rose from the dead is evidence that God exists.' Nor is this latter point semantic quibbling because if E, for the early church, entails H, as I will show that it does, then E cannot be possible evidence for H. My contention is that the early church did not draw metaphysical conclusions (at least, that God exists) from particular events (at least, that Jesus rose).

Thirdly, for E to be possible evidence that H it is necessary that there is an explanatory connection between H and E, H and E (must be true), and their probability must be greater given certain background information, K. I have shown, however, that a disjunction of alternatives (other than those Swinburne considers) that may make up K may be more probable than E. As a matter of fact, Swinburne does not consider these alternatives:

'It would not be appropriate for one who is not professionally a detective or a historian or a New Testament scholar to discuss the historical evidence for and against certain historical claims; nor is there space to do so in this book.'

I can well appreciate Swinburne's reluctance, but insofar as the historical evidence (and not just the possibility of violations of the laws of nature) is crucial to the formulation of K, then some such decision has to be made about the sub-hypotheses operating in the collecting and sorting of K. Swinburne has built a complicated edifice on crumbling foundations.

I've also argued in *The Numbers Out of the Hat* case and *The Paradox of Ideal Evidence* case that, given the notion of evidence as Swinburne employs it, an increasing probability is not sufficient for evidence and, secondly, that it is not necessary.

Insofar as Swinburne's argument suffers these three main deficiencies it fails to establish that given some such event as the resurrection of Jesus that it is likely that there is a God and, furthermore, that his claim that religious belief took this form of argument in the early church is unsubstantiated; indeed, as a matter of historical fact, it is false.

What are we to say then of the thesis which construes religious belief as belief in propositions entailing probability-related evidence? First, we should note that there are some religious beliefs we have considered, e.g., the resurrection, which are presented in the New Testament along propositional lines. These historical claims (and no doubt others) are corrigible, and believed to be so, but are presented with evidence which, it is believed, renders them probable. We have also seen that faith intends past events, therefore faith is, to that extent at least, propositional. On the other hand, we found no evidence that the early church used empirical evidence to support metaphysical conclusions in the way that Swinburne wishes to do (and so many others before him: St Thomas Aquinas, Hume, etc). Faith is not a matter of assent to propositions when it is construed as propositional assent entailing probability-related evidence statements. If belief is propositional in the way that Swinburne has argued it is, we would expect his assessment to be sustained by its application to central, and partly empirical, statements such as the ones we have been considering about the resurrection. But we have seen that the application of his argument brings up major flaws in the assessment of miracles and therefore conclude that faith is not primarily propositional in the way he suggested it is. He wants to say that propositional belief lies at the heart of all belief. He has not established his case and certainly not in relation to the New Testament.

It is appropriate, therefore, that we turn our attention, after a brief hiatus, to just what faith is.

Notes:

1. In symbols: $\Pr(H/E \,\&\, B) = \dfrac{\Pr(E/H \,\&\, B) \times \Pr(H/B)}{\Pr(E/B)}$

The probability of H, given E and B equals the probability of E given H and B times the probability of H given B over the probability of E given B.

2. pp. 225-226 in chapter 12 'Arguments from History and Miracles' in *The Existence of God,* Oxford: Clarendon, 1979.

3. Hence $P(E/H.K) > P(E/\text{-}H.K)$ and so $P(E/H.K) > P(E/K)$.

4. op. cit., pp. 236ff.

5. The examples are P. Achinstein's: 'Concept of Evidence', *Mind*, 87, 1978.

11
But first: Propositional Belief – a Joke?

1.0 Assumptions:

1.1 **Baye's Theorem**: someone who evaluates an hypothesis (H) on the basis of evidence (E) brings to its assessment:

  1.11 a prior degree of confidence in H;
  1.12 prior expectations whether E should occur if H is correct; and
  1.13 a prior degree of confidence that E should (or should not) occur regardless of whether H is true.
  1.14 In symbols:
  Pr (H/E & B) = Pr (E/H & B) x Pr (H/B)
  $\qquad\qquad\qquad$ Pr (E/B)

1.2 **The Principle of Reasonable Belief** holds:

  1.21   If, in the light of background information B, E is evidence that H, then, given B, E is at least good reason for believing H.

1.3 All probability theory evidence gathering is based on at least both Baye's Theorem and the Principle of Reasonable Belief.

1.4 **Aristotle's Axiom**: either p or not p (for

any instantiation of p you like).

1.41 In symbols: p v -p.

2.0 A probability-based proof that God exists incorporating Pascal's Wager, Baye's Theorem and the Principle of Reasonable Belief

2.1 **Pascal's Wager**: If one believes in God and God exists, then one gains infinite bliss after death. If, on the other hand, one believes in God and God does not exist, one has lost very little. However, if one does not believe in God, and God does exist, one receives infinite torment in Hell after death.

2.11 Taking the options for a wager (a wager on there being a God with the chance of infinite bliss, etc.) as having a probabilistic value of ½ for p and q (God exists and you wager) and ½ for not p (-p) and not q (-q) (-p = God does not exist and -q = you do not wager) and taking as axiomatic:

2.112 $p = \frac{1}{2}$, $-p = \frac{1}{2}$, q given $p = 7/8$ and -q, given $p = 1/8$, then, utilising Baye's Theorem:

2.113

	P. (q)	P. (-q)
P. (p)	$1_{7/16}$	$2_{1/16}$
P. (-p)	$3_{1/32}$	$4_{15/32}$

(i.e. the probability of p.q = 7/16 (= 1 x 7/8))

then:
p½ and q = 7/8
p½ and -q = 1/8
-p½ and q = 1/16
-p½ and -q = 15/16

(given p then q = 7/8)

then:

q 15/32 and p = 14/15
q 15/32 and -p = 1/15
-q 17/32 and p = 2/17
-q 17/32 and -p = 15/17

therefore:

2.115 Given that one wagered the possibility of God existing then that God exists is probable in the ratio of 14/15.
2.116 Probabilistically speaking, therefore, God exists.

3.0 A probability-based proof that God does not exist incorporating Pascal's Wager, Baye's Theorem and the Principle of Reasonable Belief

3.1 There are more possibilities than that God exists and that God does not exist. Suppose that there is a supernatural being – let us call him Lord Lucan (I choose Lord Lucan as one of an infinite variety of logically possible options only, and therefore as no more than illustrative) – who punishes with infinite torment after death anyone who believes in God or any other supernatural being (including himself) and rewards anyone who believes in no supernatural being with infinite bliss after death. Some might feel that this kind of perversity sits happily with the existential angst of modern man. Since Lord Lucan's existence is not logically impossible, then his existence is finitely probable.

3.11 To simplify matters, and according the values of 2.1 – 2.116 above, and employing both Baye's Theorem and the Principle of Reasonable Belief, then the set of logical options of the Wager can be expressed in a simple matrix:

	God exists
Believe that God exists (p)	$\infty \times p1$
Believe that Lord Lucan exists (s)	$-\infty \times p1$
Do not believe that p or s exists	$-\infty \times p1$

	Lord Lucan exists
Believe that God exists (p)	$-\infty \times p2$
Believe that Lord Lucan exists (s)	$-\infty \times p2$

Do not believe that p or s exists	∞ x p2
	Neither exists
Believe that God exists (p)	-z x p3
Believe that Lord Lucan exists (s)	-x x p3
Do not believe that p or s exists	y x p3

(the above assumes that p1 + p2 + p3 = 1)

3.12 On the above, believing in Lord Lucan would be the worst choice. The expected value would be -∞ and belief in God would be the next best. But believing in neither would be the best choice since the expected value would be y + p3 (where y is some finite utility and p3 some finite probability).

3.13 If we add to the matrix a *third* supernatural being who gives infinite reward for belief in Lord Lucan and himself and no rewards for anything else, then belief in Lord Lucan would be no worse or better than belief in God.

3.14 Therefore, given that one wagered the possibility that neither God, nor any other supernatural being exists, it is probable that God does not exist in the ratio of whatever one instantiates in the variables y and p.

3.15 Probabilistically-speaking, therefore, God does not exist.

4.0 Conclusions

4.1 From 2.116 above and 3.15 above, we get both:

4.11 Probabilistically speaking, God exists
and
4.12 Probabilistically speaking, God does not exist.
4.13 In symbols:
    both p and not p.

4.2 Now this offends Aristotle's axiom (and common sense) that:
Not both p and not p
usually expressed:
either p or not p.

5.0 As Henry Ford almost certainly did not say: probability is bunk. Or as Cicero almost said: the people judge a few things by their truth, and many by probability (*Vulgus ex veritate pauca, ex opinione multa aestimat*).

12
What is Faith?

'And now abideth faith, hope, charity (Greek: *agape* = love), these three; but the greatest of these is charity' (1 *Corinthians* 13: 13). Like hope and love, faith is a virtue: in essence, it is trust. Faith (Greek: *pistis* often wrongly translated as 'belief') was, in the early church, a form of commitment, trust, or loyalty. In the New Testament, the word is concerned mainly with a personal relationship established by trust. There is not one instance where it is said that x 'has faith that...', where the object clause is taken in the propositional sense. Faith, essentially, was a transforming personal experience.

Bultmann suggests that the rare occurrences of 'faith' in the Synoptics (*Matthew*, *Mark* and *Luke*) derived ultimately from the early church rather than from the lips of Jesus. Where it does occur, it is always in response to Jesus' proclamation and is usually linked with miracles. In the Synoptics, miracles are significant: all who turn to Jesus in faith to ask for healing count on his power when all else has failed. The miracle stories are meant to show that Jesus does not disregard the faith of those who trust his power. Faith thus becomes the opposite of all doubt and, conversely, where

Jesus does not find faith he can 'do no miracle'. This notion of faith as trust in God's power has its roots in the Old Testament. Of 'faith' in the Synoptics, Jeremias says: 'The saying about the faith that can move mountains... indicates the significance Jesus attaches to faith.... The decisive feature for understanding [the illustration] is that the disappearance of mountains and their reappearance to support the mountain of God was expected as an eschatological event. Even the weakest kind of faith, as tiny as a grain of mustard seed, will – so Jesus promises – not primarily perform spectacular miracles, so much as have a share in the eschatological consummation.'[1]

In the Gospel of *John*, we find that faith means an attitude, not an intellectual agreement with the content of belief; it is a response to the divine action seen in Jesus.

In Paul, faith is a consequence of God's soteriological act in the life of Jesus. Because it is tied to his life and death and because this is communicated in preaching, faith comes about by hearing the Word (Greek: *kerygma* = preaching). For Paul, faith is not an intellectual state of affairs but obedience.

In the New Testament, the keywords which characterise the notion of faith are: response (commitment/assent), trust, and obedience. As HH Farmer says: '... the proper response to revelation is faith, faith being not an intellectual assent to general truths, but the decisive commitment of the whole person in active obedience to, and... trust in, the divine will apprehended as rightfully sovereign and utterly trustworthy at one and the same time.'[2]

Notes:

1. pp. 165-166, *Theology of the New Testament*, Vol. 1, SCM, 1971.
2. p. 88, *The World and God*, Nisbet, 1936.

13
Faith in Jesus

In religion, faith is the principal virtue: faith in God, faith in Christianity, faith in Jesus. In the latter case, this is faith in a long dead person mediated by the detritus of history. As such, faith in Jesus is defeasible and subject to the rigours of historical disciplines. But how is it possible to move from an unattainable history of the man Jesus to faith in Christ? How can one traverse this 'broad, ugly ditch' as Lessing describes it? Or how can one deal with the problem of *The Disciple at Second Hand*, identified by Kierkegaard?

Lessing

Gotthold Ephraim Lessing (1729 – 81) was a German philosopher, art critic and dramatist; he was more inclined to the theatre than he was to the lecture hall.

Born in Kamenz in Saxony, he went to the University of Leipzig where he took a degree in theology, medicine, philosophy and philology. Here he began a relationship with the famous German actress, Karoline Neuber. In 1748 – 1760, he lived in Leipzig and Berlin while, in 1752, he did a Master's in Wittenberg; somewhere in the interim Karoline disappeared from his life.

From 1760 – 1765, he worked in Breslau as secretary to General Tanentzien during the Seven Years War. From 1767 – 1770, he worked at Hamburg National Theatre, Germany's first national theatre. It was here that he met Eva Konig who was later to become his wife. In 1770, he became librarian under the Duke of Brunswick at the ducal library, now the *Herzog August Biliothek*, in Wolfenbuttel. Here he joined the *Zu den drei Goldenen Rosen* lodge of the Freemasons.

Lessing married Eva in 1776 and she died, giving birth to a short-lived son, in 1778. On 15 February, 1781, Lessing died during a visit to a wine dealer.

Lessing was a friend of the philosopher Moses Mendelssohn, grandfather to Felix. For a short time, his theological/philosophical works were banned.

In the spirit of the Enlightenment, and particularly of Spinoza and the Deists, Lessing, in his essay *On the Proof of the Spirit and of Power*, sharply delineated what he calls the 'broad, ugly ditch' between acceptance of an historical narrative and true religious conviction. The essays are in reply to JD Schumann's *On the Evidence of the Proofs for the Truth of the Christian Religion*, which is a standard orthodox defence of the verbal infallibility of Scripture (largely provoked by Reimarus' attack; Reimarus was a friend of Lessing). Schumann based his argument on

Origen's discussion of 'the proof of the spirit and of power'.

Lessing's essay deals with the nature and strength of the evidence that may be adduced in support of religious doctrine. It represents a forceful attack on what was once taken for granted by many to provide a firm foundation for the truths of Christian doctrine.

Lessing rejects all historical proofs of the Christian religion but he endeavours to show that its truth, taken as a body of doctrine and ethic, may be found to be true independently of any historical considerations. He begins his essay with the distinction between fulfilled prophecies and miracles, and historical reports of fulfilled prophecies and miracles. Whilst the former, when actually experienced, may have given the assurance of certainty and proof to the witnesses, the latter can do no such thing:

'Fulfilled prophecies, which I myself experience, are one thing; fulfilled prophecies, of which I know only from history that others say they have experienced them, are another. Miracles which I see with my own eyes, and which I have the opportunity to verify for myself, are one thing; miracles which I know only from history that others say they have seen and verified them, are another.
That, surely, is beyond controversy?'[1]

Lessing accepts that, at the time of Jesus, the proof of the spirit and of power may well have retained its strength; and if he were present then and had no doubts that these miracles were true, he says 'I would have gained so much confidence that I would have willingly submitted my intellect to his [Christ's], and I would have believed him in all things in which equally indisputable experiences did not tell against him'. Furthermore, this would be so if the 'believing Christians' were able in his own time to perform such works as Christ. But this is not so:

'I am no longer in Origen's position; I live in the eighteenth century, in which miracles no longer happen.'

Lessing seems to regret that he is left in an age in which no immediate certainty is available and which is left with nothing but historical narratives of these events. Despite the fact that there is nothing but these narratives left, many, like Schumann, persist in using them as the foundation for arguments for the truth of the Christian religion. It is against this endeavour that Lessing argues. The problem is:

'... the proof is now entirely lapsed; if, then, historical certainty is much too weak to replace this apparent proof which has lapsed: how is it to be expected of me that the same inconceivable truths which sixteen to eighteen hundred years ago people believed on the strongest inducement, should be believed by me to be equally valid on an infinitely lesser inducement?'[2]

The Enlightenment was not unaware of degrees of certainty obtainable from rational demonstration, direct experience, and testimony. And this, for Lessing, constituted his central problem. Few would argue that the historical narratives would deal the same degree of certainty as rational demonstrations or immediate experience, but what Lessing finds contentious is:

'What is asserted is that the reports alone which we have of these prophecies and miracles are as reliable as historical truths ever can be. And then it is added that historical truths cannot be demonstrated: nevertheless we must believe them as firmly as truths that have been demonstrated.'

Lessing believes that, while no one will deny that the reports of these miracles and prophecies are as reliable as historical truths ever can be, they are nevertheless treated as if they were infinitely more reliable. Furthermore, what does it mean to accept an historical proposition as true:

'Does it mean anything other than this: to accept this proposition, this truth as valid? To accept that there is no objection to be brought against it? To accept that one historical proposition is built on one thing, another on another, that from one historical truth another follows? To reserve to oneself the right to estimate other historical things accordingly? Does it mean anything other than this? Anything more?'

So while, as it seems for the sake of argument, Lessing is willing to accept that historical facts brought in support of the Christian faith are reliable, he will not acquiesce in like manner to the inferences that the theologians of his day were prone to draw from such facts:

'If on historical grounds I have no objection to the statement that Christ himself rose from the dead, must I therefore accept it as true that that risen Christ was the Son of God?'[3]

While Lessing may have no objection to the historical claims of Christianity, e.g., the resurrection, or even the Jesus claimed to be the Son of God, it does not follow that religious dogmas based on these facts are true. Again, in the spirit of Spinoza, he argues:

'... to jump without historical truth to a quite different class of truths, and to demand of me that I should form all my metaphysical and moral ideas of the nature of the Godhead because I cannot set any credible testimony against the resurrection of Christ: if that is not a *metabasis eis allo genos* [change into another category] then I do not know what Aristotle meant by that phrase.'

But while Lessing's work here resembles that of Spinoza and the Deists, he does differ in some fundamental aspects in the conclusions he derives from his argument. The basic difference being that, while he rejects the historical foundation of Christianity, he accepts the content of Christian doctrine. The conclusion of this brief paper has a distinctly positive side to it. In the same positive standpoint to the 'counter assertions' to Reimarus' *Fragments* and *The Education of the Human Race*, Lessing states what, in fact, does bind him to the Christian faith:

'Nothing but these teachings themselves. Eighteen hundred years ago they were so new, so alien, so foreign to the entire mass of truths recognised in that age, that nothing less than miracles and fulfilled prophecies were required, if the multitude were to attend them at all.'[4]

Thus the miracles and fulfilled prophecies served as the occasions for the reception of these new and alien truths. We now possess the fruits. What more do we need?:

'These fruits I may see before me ripe and ripened, and may I not be satisfied with that? The old pious legend that the hand which scatters the seed must wash in snails' blood seven times for each throw, I do not doubt, but merely ignore it. What does it matter to me whether the legend is false or true? The fruits are excellent. Suppose that a very useful mathematical truth had been reached by the discoverer through an obvious fallacy. (Even if such an instance does not exist, yet it could). Should I deny this truth? Should I refuse to use this truth? Would I be on that account an ungrateful reviler of the discoverer, if I were unwilling to prove from his insight in other respects, indeed, did not consider it capable of proof, that the fallacy through which he stumbled upon the truth could not be a fallacy?'

Indeed, the mature Lessing came to argue that the Christian religion possessed an 'inner truth' and because of this it may be evaluated and appreciated independently of all factual, historical considerations. Thus the Gospel narratives, the Scripture, the miracles, become merely the occasion by which this inner truth is communicated. In support of this distinction, Lessing made his most famous assertion that 'the accidental truths of history can never become the proof of necessary truths of reason'. Thus, while historical events may suggest or occasion religious truths, they can never legitimise them. From this, it follows, according to Lessing, that the Christian religion is not true because of the contingent fact that the apostles happened to teach it; but quite the reverse: they taught it because of its inner truth. Thus Lessing has raised important questions about the relation between historical truth and religious truths.

But is it really the case that what is believed about God must be a 'necessary truth of reason'? In saying that he accepts Christianity on the strength of the teachings themselves, he renders redundant any need for the historical Jesus. Lessing's argument amounts to showing that any Christian belief about God could *not* be derived from historical propositions; a precursor to a Barthian reaction to the Jesus of history. Moreover, Lessing is simply wrong to say that historical certainty can never be adequate for absolute certainty: there are only too many historical facts of which we can be absolutely certain: there was a second world war. We know *absolutely* a great many such things. It is silly to subjugate the certainty of the historical to the certainty of the experiential as a matter of course.

Of Lessing's argument here, Elizabeth Anscombe says:

'What is to be believed about God, about what can be ascribed to God, he thinks of as a "necessary truth of reason", a metaphysical truth, I suppose; and a metaphysical truth, like a mathematical truth, could not possibly *follow* from a historical fact: if it could follow, then the historical fact would have to be as certain as metaphysical truths are supposed to be; but a historical fact *could* be quite uncertain... I think it is not worth attention, because the assumption that anything believable about God must be "a necessary truth of reason" is worse than doubtful; it is incoherent.'[5]

I don't think Anscombe is so much concerned here with whether a necessary truth could not possibly follow from an historical fact. As her daughter, Mary Geach, tells us in the introduction to *Faith in a Hard Ground*, Anscombe realised that of course one can derive necessary conclusions from contingent premises. Geach, in criticising Russell, says: '... from a contingent conjunction of the form "all a's are b's and all b's are a's" we get a necessary conclusion of the form "all a's are a's", which follows here neither because it is a necessary proposition presupposed by the premises, nor because, being necessary, it is implied by all propositions, but by the application to a contingent premise of rules... which we all use to deduce contingent propositions from one another.'[6] No, Anscombe's concern is about the way in which we come to know about God and when we look and see how this happens then the assumption that anything believable about God must be a necessary truth of reason becomes obviously incoherent.

The point of this problem, however, has been demonstrated even more acutely by Kierkegaard, who was much exercised by the relation of what he calls the 'eternal' to the 'temporal'.

Kierkegaard

Soren Kierkegaard (1813 – 55), frail and always sickly, was a strange man who came to be known as the Melancholy Dane. He declared himself to be 'infinitely pugnacious' and, as a consequence, was bullied at school. The youngest of seven, he lost his mother and five of his siblings before he was 21. While writing his Master's dissertation, *On the Concept of Irony with Constant Reference to Socrates*, he pined for Regina Olsen, a young woman aged 16. He had to overcome considerable opposition from her family and also the affections of a rival suitor and all of this in spite of the fact that she was already engaged to Fritz Schlegel.

In exasperation, Regina finally broke the engagement to Fritz and in September 1840, Soren and Regina announced their engagement. Sadly, on the night of their engagement, Kierkegaard discovered that he preferred Regina in her absence; he had made a bad mistake: falling in love with love itself. But if *he* broke the engagement this would lead to *her* everlasting shame. He determined to corral her into breaking their engagement and thus decided to treat her badly; both of them suffered. In October 1841, Regina broke the engagement.

Having, in 1841, attended lectures by Schelling in Berlin, Kierkegaard became a trenchant critic of Hegel (1770 – 1831), one of philosophy's most impenetrable practitioners. Indeed, he saw Hegel as one of the two great enemies of Christianity, the other being the unthinking church-goer.

Kierkegaard often wrote pseudonymously. Throughout his life he toyed with the idea of entering the priesthood. He was left as a figure of public ridicule following the publication of vituperative articles about him in a satirical weekly, *The Corsair*. In his last few years, and having spent most of the considerable fortune that he inherited, he frittered away the rest on an incendiary broadsheet, *The Instant*, relentlessly attacking the state church and all things ecclesiastical.

In October 1855, Kierkegaard fell in the street, paralysed. He lived for a further month while well-intentioned friends tried to persuade him to recant his attacks on the church. Obdurate, Kierkegaard refused. He also refused the last sacrament offered by a priest, averring that he should send a layman to administer the host, not some flunky of the state. On 11 November 1855, Kierkegaard died.

It transpired that while a dying Kierkegaard was resisting the blandishments of those who would bring him back 'into the fold' – and in so doing vitiate much of his life's work – a well-organised funeral had been planned at which Peter, his remaining sibling, would apologise for his brother. While the service took place in a crowded church, university students rioted in protest outside and the service was interrupted by his nephew protesting against the appropriation by the Danish Church of a man who fundamentally opposed it.

Heidegger's (1889 – 1976) debt to Kierkegaard is not to be underestimated and Wittgenstein (1889 – 1951) called him 'by far the most profound thinker of the last century'.

Kierkegaard's *Philosophical Fragments* and *Concluding Unscientific Postscript* represent an attack on speculative Idealism. The motto on Kierkegaard's title page of the *Fragments* asks:

'Is an historical point of departure possible for an eternal consciousness; how can such a point of departure have any other than a merely historical interest; is it possible to base an eternal happiness on historical knowledge?'

It is in this manner that Kierkegaard poses the question which Lessing first raised concerning the relationship between revelation and history and also the problem made more important by Hegel and his disciples, of the relationship between revelation and reason. Kierkegaard begins the *Fragments* with a preface that sets the climate for what is to follow: his pseudonymous works are depictions of certain aspects of life and are, therefore, in one sense, caricatures. He is concerned with the moral, the aesthetic and the religious. In discussing these, he reaches a tension which forces him to take account of another dimension: the aesthetic reaches a tension where the moral takes over, and so on.

In the first question of the *Fragments*, he asks, 'How far does the truth admit of being learned?' He answers the question by reference to Socrates and the doctrine of 'recollection'. For Socrates, all learning was only a matter of recollecting what was already known by the learner but latent or forgotten. The teacher thus becomes merely the occasion for the learning and, as an occasion, the historical starting point for learning is a matter of indifference. However, if teaching the truth is to be something other than Socrates maintained, how then is it to be different? The point of decisive significance is to be found, Kierkegaard notes, in the Moment of Time. This is so because 'the eternal which hitherto did not exist, came into existence at this moment'. On the basis of this assumption, certain conclusions can be drawn with regard to the antecedent state and the teacher. As regards the former, the learner in this case will be such, not that the truth is latent in him, but that he does not know the truth. Recollection does not apply here:

'He must therefore be characterised as beyond the pale of Truth, not approaching it like a proselyte but departing from it; or as being in Error. He is then in a state of Error.'[7]

THE ANATOMY OF BELIEF AND UNBELIEF

As regards the latter, the teacher will not only have to give the latter the truth but will also have to create the condition for its reception:

'Now if the learner is to acquire the truth, the Teacher must bring it to him; and not only so, but he must also give him the condition necessary for understanding it. For, if the learner were in his own person the condition for understanding the Truth, he need only recall it. The condition for understanding the Truth is like the capacity to inquire for it: the condition contains the conditioned, and the question implies the answer.'[8]

The learner was created by God with the condition for the reception of truth but has, by his own fault, thrown it away. This may be called a state of Sin. The teacher, who creates the condition in the learner for recovering the truth, and brings him the truth, may be called a Saviour, Redeemer, or Judge; and the moment in which he imparts his lesson, when the Temporal is filled with the Eternal, may be called the Fullness of Time.

After, he deals with the subject of God as Teacher and Redeemer, and with the manner in which the learner may be taught the eternal without being annihilated, and with what he called 'The Absolute Paradox': it is folly to try to prove the existence of God because any proof assumes the existence of what is called into question, for 'merely to obtain the knowledge that the God is unlike him, man needs the help of the God; and now he learns that the God is absolutely different, this cannot be accounted for on the basis of what man derives from the God, for insofar they are akin'[9]. Kierkegaard then passes to the subject of 'The Contemporary Disciple' and 'The Disciple at Second Hand'.

In order to learn of the Eternal, the learner must be made to feel himself to be nothing, without being annihilated. He must feel he owes everything to God, and yet be able to approach God freely. There is but one way in which this can be achieved: if the Teacher becomes like the learner and appears in the form of a servant. The Contemporary Disciple is one who is historically contemporary with God's presence in the form of a servant among men. However, the presence of the teacher in the form of a servant is not only a necessary part for laying down the conditions in which the lesson may be learned, it is an essential part of the lesson itself:

'... the God's presence is not accidental in relation to his teaching, but essential. The God's presence in human form, aye, in the humble form of a servant, is itself the Teaching, and the God must give the condition along with it ... or the learner will understand nothing.'[10]

The contemporary has no difficulty in becoming an eyewitness, but that does not make him a disciple:

'Though a contemporary readily becomes an historical eyewitness, the difficulty is that the knowledge of some historical circumstances, or, indeed, a knowledge of all the circumstances with the reliability of an eyewitness, does not make such an eyewitness a disciple; which is apparent from the fact that this knowledge has merely historical significance for him. We see at once that the historical in the more concrete sense is a matter of indifference; we may suppose a degree of ignorance with respect to it, and permit this ignorance as if to annihilate one detail after the other, historically annihilating the historical; if only the Moment remains, as point of departure for the Eternal, the paradox will be there.'[11]

Thus, as long as the historical moment remains a starting point for the eternal, concrete historical detail does not matter. What does matter is the Teacher:

'Faith is not a form of knowledge; for all knowledge is either knowledge of the Eternal, excluding the temporal and historical as indifferent, or it is pure historical knowledge. No knowledge can have for its object the absurdity that the Eternal is the historical. If I know Spinoza's doctrine, then I am insofar not concerned with Spinoza but with his doctrine; at some other time I may be concerned historically with Spinoza himself. But the disciple is in faith so related to his Teacher as to be eternally concerned with his historical existence.'[12]

Immediate contemporaneity can only be an occasion for obtaining historical knowledge; for receiving the condition which makes faith possible; for Socratic self-study. But if the Socratic assumption is dropped and it is assumed that the Teacher himself contributes the condition to the learner, then the object of faith is not the teaching but the Teacher. With such a Teacher, real contemporaneity does not depend on any merely temporal relationship. Thus a learner in a later generation may possibly be contemporary with his Teacher.

The final chapter of the *Fragments* deals with the problem of the Disciple at Second Hand. There is no basic difference in the situation of the generation contemporary with the Teacher and the generation that has had his lesson passed on at second hand, except that the first is closer to the immediate certainty of the historical fact of the Eternal coming in the Fullness of Time as a servant; whereas the latter generation is more able to assess the historical consequences of this fact. Basically, Kierkegaard concludes, these learners have an equal footing.

To provide what he calls an 'orientation' in dealing with the way in which God is coming into time may be considered, Kierkegaard distinguishes three ways this coming may be construed:

a) if it is a simple historical fact 'contemporaneity is a desideratum';
b) if it is an eternal fact then 'every age is equally near';
c) if it is an absolute fact (as Kierkegaard has argued it is) then 'it would be a contradiction to suppose that time had any power to differentiate the fortunes of men with respect to it...'.[13]

But the absolute fact is an historical fact and as such it is the object of faith. Nevertheless, although the historical gives the occasion for the contemporary to become a disciple, it is only through God himself that the condition of discipleship is received. And this does not depend on contemporaneity. The consequence of this is that:

'... there is no disciple at second hand. The first and the last are essentially on the same plane, only that a later generation finds its occasion in the testimony of the previous generation, while the contemporary generation finds this occasion in its own immediate contemporaneity, and, insofar owes nothing to any other generation. But this immediate contemporaneity is merely an occasion which can scarcely be expressed more emphatically than in the proposition that the disciple, if he understood himself, must wish that the immediate contemporaneity should cease, by the God's leaving the earth.'[14]

The Fragments are only properly understood in the light of Kierkegaard's following, and according to him, his most significant, literary work, *The Concluding Unscientific Postscript. The Postscript*, as Kierkegaard says in his preface, is not simply a continuation of the *Fragments*, but an attempt to treat the same problem in a different way.

The Postscript is divided into two books; the first book deals with 'The Objective Problem Concerning the Truth of Christianity'. In the 'Introductory Remarks', Kierkegaard notes:

'From an objective standpoint, Christianity is a *res in facto posita* [lit.: placed the thing in the thing made], whose truth it is proposed to investigate in a purely objective manner for the accommodating subject is much too objective not to leave himself out; or perhaps he even unhesitatingly counts himself in, as one who possesses faith as a matter of course. The truth in this objective sense may mean, first, the historical truth; second, the philosophical truth.'[15]

The way in which the historical truth in Christianity must be determined is by critical examination of various records, i.e., the methods of other fields of historical enquiry also apply in the field of the enquiry into the historical truth of Christianity. However, if one is concerned about the philosophical truth of Christianity, then it is the relationship of the historically given doctrine to the eternal truth one must consider.

In Book 1, Kierkegaard argues, in shades reminiscent of Flaubert's *Madame Bovary*, that the attempt to provide an objective proof of the truth of Christianity is misguided:

'Here is the crux of the matter, and I come back to the case of learned theology. For whose sake is it that the proof is sought? Faith does not need it; aye, it must even regard proof as its enemy. But when faith begins to feel embarrassed and ashamed, like a woman for whom her love is no longer sufficient but who secretly feels ashamed of her lover and must therefore have it established that there is something remarkable about him – then faith begins to lose its passion, when faith begins to cease to be faith, then a proof becomes necessary so as to command respect from the side of unbelief.'[16]

It is in this way that proof, whether based on the Bible, the church, or the proof of the centuries, is misguided. Such proofs are irrelevant because, 'Christianity is spirit, spirit is inwardness, inwardness is subjectivity, subjectivity is essentially passion, and in its maximum an infinite, personal, passionate interest in one's eternal happiness.'[17]

In Book II, Part 1, Kierkegaard deals with Lessing's

paper *On the Proof of the Spirit and of Power*, and considers the quote that 'accidental historical truths can never serve as proofs for eternal truths of reason' in relation to his own problem of the *Fragments*, viz. is it possible to base an eternal happiness on historical knowledge? Of Lessing's paper, he notes:

'Lessing opposes what I would call an attempt to create a quantitative transition to a qualitative decision. He attacks the direct transition from historical trustworthiness to the determination of an eternal happiness. He does not deny, for he knows how to make concessions so as to make the category stand out more clearly, that the accounts of miracles and prophecies found in the scriptures are as reliable, as other historical testimony, as reliable as historical testimony in general is capable of being. But now, seeing that they are only so reliable, why is it proposed to make use of them that demands an infinitely greater reliability?'[18]

Inasmuch as Lessing opposes himself, Kierkegaard notes, to the simple and direct transition from the reliability of an historical account to an eternal decision, he adopts the position of drawing a distinction between historical testimony relating to miracles and prophecies, and contemporaneity with such things. The great difference between Lessing on the one hand, and Kierkegaard on the other, lies in the fact that, for the latter, 'there can in all eternity be no direct transition from the historical to the eternal, whether the historical is contemporary or not.'[19]

Foreshadowing Wittgenstein, we find, in Kierkegaard, that faith is not the outcome of ratiocination: historical certainty is unobtainable; but faith does not doubt; probability has no place in a faith which provides the basis for eternal happiness so faith cannot be based on history. Moreover, faith requires, even more, faith *is* passion which demands that we embrace the improbability of belief. Perversely, one might think, this passion appealed to the existentialist atheists Karl Jaspers and Jean-Paul Sartre but also the modern Protestant theologian Karl Barth. Jaspers, in *The Psychology of World-Views* (1919), was the first to identify the similarities between the work of Kierkegaard and that of Nietzsche. Existentialism had its roots in German Romanticism in its concern for individualism against the rationality of the eighteenth-century Enlightenment, but Kierkegaard was its forerunner.

William James

William James (1842 – 1910), brother of Henry James the novelist, was a Harvard professor of psychology and philosophy who for the Gifford Lectures, delivered in 1901, wrote *The Varieties of Religious Experience*, published in 1902.

Born in New York, James was educated in America and Europe where he acquired fluency in French and German. He graduated from Harvard Medical School in 1869 where, after a time of ill-health and depression, he became an instructor in anatomy and physiology at Harvard. His interest in psychology led to his *Principles of Psychology* published in 1890; it became a standard text in the field. In 1879, he started lectures at Harvard on philosophy leading, in 1885, to his becoming a Professor of Philosophy. In 1897, he published *The Will to Believe and Other Essays in Popular Philosophy* followed by *Pragmatism* (1907), *A Pluralistic Universe* and *The Meaning of Truth* (1909) and, posthumously, *Some Problems of Philosophy* and *Memories and Studies* (1911) and *Essays in Radical Empiricism* (1912) followed later by various letters, reviews and essays. He was an affable man and a captivating speaker.

In a letter, James wrote of his book *The Varieties of Religious Experience*: 'The problem I have set myself is a hard one: first, to defend... "experience" against "philosophy" as being the real backbone of the world's religious life, what I myself invincibly do believe, that, although all the special manifestations of religion may have been absurd (I mean its creeds and theories), yet the life of it as a whole is mankind's most important function.'[20]

James is generally known as a radical empiricist or

pragmatist, essentially, we can go no further than experience. And *The Varieties* shows no interest in propositional belief, metaphysics or doctrine. He is interested in religion for what it has to say about 'what goes on in the single private man' in terms of his 'intimate needs, ideals, desolations, consolations, failures, successes.' Religion is 'the feelings, acts, and experiences of individual men in their solitude, so far as they apprehend themselves to stand in relation to whatever they may consider divine.' The rest: 'theologies, philosophies and ecclesiastical organisations' are secondary. John Gray sees *The Varieties* as 'the best book ever written on religion by a philosopher'.[21]

After rehearsing an extensive range of 'extreme' and 'extravagant' case studies (including his own reported anonymously), James concludes: 'So long as we deal with the cosmic and the general, we deal only with the symbols of reality, but *as soon as we deal with private and personal phenomena as such, we deal with realities in the completest sense of the term*'[22]. And: 'When we survey the whole field of religion, we find a great variety in the thoughts that have prevailed there, but the feelings on the one hand and the conduct on the other are almost always the same, for Stoic, Christian, and Buddhist saints are practically indistinguishable in their lives. The theories which religion generates, being thus variable, are secondary; and if you wish to grasp her essence, you must look to the feelings and the conduct as being the more constant elements. It is between these two elements that the short-circuit exists on which she carries on her principal business, while the ideas and symbols and other institutions form loop lines: ... which are not to be regarded as organs with an indispensable function, necessarily at all times for religious life to go on'.[23]

Faith is 'among the forces by which men live' and holds 'a very minimum of intellectual content'.

James provides a way out of the impasse addressed in their different ways by Lessing and Kierkegaard: by simply *looking and seeing* into the lives of the faithful he offers an insight into the nature of what it is to believe.

For Lessing, as we have seen, no amount of historical evidence is sufficient to justify conclusions about necessary truths relating to the Divine.

For Kierkegaard, faith is not the outcome of reason. 'Is it possible to base an eternal happiness upon historical knowledge?' No, he says: firstly, no amount of history can deliver certainty and faith cannot live with doubt. Secondly, the natural development of historical research carries with it an open-endedness inimical to a wholehearted religious commitment. Thirdly, faith is inwardness, it is passion, it is not the disinterested study of historical texts.

For James, experience, or feeling, constitutes the foundation of reality. Pre-figuring the work of the later Wittgenstein, James sees his task as primarily descriptive: truth is not a conceptual copy of reality. All that philosophy can do is assist in the articulation of religious experience. We should regard the language in which it consists as tools for dealing with reality rather than as revealing essences. James, rightly, had little time for the metaphysical in religion.

Notes:

1. p. 51, H. Chadwick, *Lessing's Theological Writing*, A & C Black, 1956.
2. *op. cit., p. 53.*
3. *op. cit., p. 54.*
4. *op. cit., p. 55.*
5. *p. 23, Faith in a Hard Ground, Imprint Academic, 2008.*
6. *op. cit., p. xvii.*
7. *pp. 16-17, translated D Swenson, Princeton University, 1974.*
8. *op. cit., pp. 17-18.*
9. *op. cit., p. 58.*
10. *op. cit., pp. 68-69.*
11. *op. cit., 73-74.*
12. *op. cit., p. 76.*
13. *op. cit., p. 125.*
14. *op. cit., pp. 131-132.*

15. *p. 23, translated D Swenson, Princeton University, 1944.*
16. *op. cit., p. 31.*
17. *op. cit., p. 33.*
18. *op. cit., p. 88.*
19. *op. cit., p. 89.*
20. p. xix, *The Varieties of Religious Experience*, Penguin, 1982.
21. p. 2, *Seven Types of Atheism.*
22. *op. cit.* p. 498.
23. *op. cit.* p. 504.

14
Miracles

As we have seen, the question of 'miracles and prophecies' played an important role in both Lessing and Kierkegaard's deliberations. But in the sea of belief and unbelief, miracles are a red herring.

There are two ways in which the concept of miracles has been construed: as coincidences and as violations of the laws of nature; both notions are, if not incoherent, morally flawed.

Coincidence Miracles

A coincidence miracle is one where there is no apparent violation of the laws of nature but where coincidences are such that they could not be described, without confusion, as non-miraculous events.

The original connotation of 'miracle' can be found in the Latin *mirari* (to be surprised at, or, to wonder). Often miracles are construed as events that do no more than excite or inspire wonder. However, inasmuch as all events may, on the theistic conception of things, be related to the divine providence, all acts may in one way or another be said to be the action of God; and insofar as this may excite wonder, or amaze, they may be called miracles. Thus, both the resurrection of Jesus and the falling rain could, on this view, be called miraculous.

If 'miracle' is applicable to every class of event and, in some cases, even further to every thing, then the word has lost any substantive content either as that which excites wonder, on the one hand, or as the action of God, on the other. To put it another way: if,

1. everything is a miracle, and,
2. miracles excite wonder, then, (from (1) and (2))
3. everything excites wonder.
So, by substitution in (1) above,
4. that which excites wonder excites wonder.

This does not seem to me to be a very significant tautology.

Roy Holland tells the story of a small child riding a toy car. He strays onto an unguarded railway crossing. The child on the track is obscured from the view of the driver of the approaching train. The train, however, comes to a halt within a few feet of the child. There was nothing supernatural about the manner in which the brakes of the train came to be applied: the driver had fainted and this was due to an exceptionally heavy lunch and a quarrel he had with a colleague, which in turn had caused a rise in his blood pressure. From the story of coincidences, Holland concludes:

'Unlike the coincidence between the rise of the Ming dynasty and the dynasty of Lancaster, the coincidence of the child's presence on the line with the arrival of and then stopping of the train is impressive, significant; not because it is very unusual for trains to be halted in the way this one was, but because the life of the child was imperilled, and then, against expectation, preserved. The significance of some coincidences as opposed to others arises from the relation to human needs and hopes and fears, their effects for good or ill upon our lives. So we speak of our luck (fortune, fate, etc.). And the kind of thing that, outside religion, we call luck is in religious parlance the grace of God or a miracle of God... But though a coincidence can be taken religiously as a sign and called a miracle and made the subject of a vow, it cannot without confusion be taken as a sign of divine interference with the natural order.'[1]

To render an event explicable by what Holland calls in this case 'historical explanation' is to render it explicable, and it is this which would not only be impropitious for the apologist but also self-defeating. If the nature of the event is such that it 'cannot without confusion be taken as a sign of divine interference with the natural order', it cannot then be taken as divine, unless the action God is elliptical for the workings of nature, history, luck; call it what you will.

If the action of God is so understood, we find ourselves in the position where we have an event that may excite or amaze us, but which, if viewed as the action of God, is vacuous.

If events admit of historical or natural explanation yet are called 'miracles', then their only claim to fame as a class of events which are different from others, i.e. as miracles, will be that they are wondrous or exciting or coincidental. How would one determine which events are wondrous, exciting, coincidental enough to qualify as miracles? Suppose we add a little to Holland's story of the child on the railway crossing and stipulate that the driver of the train had the big meal and a quarrel with his colleague, not on the same day as this incident, but several days before, and that he had fainted whilst driving on several occasions prior to the incident with the child. Will the story then be a little less miraculous? Suppose further that the train stopped, not a few feet away from the child but twenty feet, or even twenty yards. Does the element of the miraculous depend on the number of feet away from the child that the train stopped? The greater the distance put between the child and the train, the less efficacious the miracle becomes, until the train is so far away that the story doesn't even rate a telling because its wonder-value is negligible. It would seem that in such cases the criterion for the evaluation of the wonder of the thing is: the greater the incidence of the coincidences of apparently unrelated incidents that compose the overall scheme of the necessary 'historical' explanation. Yet inasmuch as it admits of this explanation it is ascribable to forces other than God: to big meals, quarrels, unattended children, high blood pressure, etc.

Nor could it be sustained, as Holland contends, that the significance of the event called miraculous is so because of the relation to human needs, hopes and fears of some coincidences as opposed to others. The general relation so many events, both wondrous and not so wondrous, to so many human aspirations and needs (which may be called luck, fate, coincidence, etc.) would suggest that there are other criteria by which the distinctiveness of a miraculous event is understood.

Coincidence miracles face the more general challenge to do with the quality and quantity of morally good coincidences as opposed to morally disastrous ones. What if, to expand Holland's story the other way, the front wheels of the train had come to rest on top of the child. Would *that* be consistent with the nature of the Deity? Would *that* be allowed to count *against* the action or involvement of supernatural forces, as the safe outcome of the story is allowed to count *for* it? If not, why not? It is not difficult to regard the idea of coincidence miracles as morally reprehensible.

THE ANATOMY OF BELIEF AND UNBELIEF

Another problem one encounters with the coincidence concept of the miraculous has to do with the religious significance of such coincidences. What is it for a coincidence to have religious significance? It might be suggested that the coincidence is of such a kind that it is consistent with the supposed nature of the Deity or, alternatively, that it occurs in a context which is specifically religious (both suggestions endorsed by Swinburne). In both cases, it will be necessary that the event which is characterised as miraculous is, at least, unlikely. If this were not the case, then the event would not be notable and 'seeing' in this instance would be devoid of content.

While I contend that coincidences cannot coherently be called miracles, it might well be the case that the believer wishes to maintain that, nevertheless, God was acting in the coincidence, that God arranged things to happen that way by design, not that they just came about. But where in the range of coincidences does one locate the point at which it makes sense to say 'God did this', or 'Unless God did things this way, we would not have had the resultant miracle?'

On the other hand, it might be argued that some coincidences, like Holland's story, are part of the whole course and workings of nature which was originally set in motion by God. Thus the mother of the story might want to claim that it was part of God's divinely pre-ordained plan that her child should be saved. Furthermore, the nature of the occurrence, it could be argued, is in keeping with the revealed nature of God, as we have seen Swinburne wants to do. This kind of argument encounters several difficulties, one being that mentioned above, that miraculous claims might easily end up being vacuous. Secondly, it faces the difficulty of explaining how the nature of God, with which these events have been identified as consistent, has been revealed. The revelation cannot easily be said itself to issue in like events, for that would end in a quandary of circularity: the religious significance of other events cannot be adduced in support of event x to show that x is consistent with the nature of God because it is precisely the religious significant of *any* event that is in question here.

The problem then becomes seeing how God can act in coincidence miracles without them becoming either what appear, to all intents and purposes, violation miracles, or what, on the other hand, make everything that happens into an act of God.

Violation Miracles

A part of David Hume's legacy to the philosophy of religion was the definition of a miracle as a violation of the laws of nature. Hume's essay on miracles is deeply flawed and does not sit happily with his general philosophical position, but that need not detain us here.

Laws of nature are descriptions of regular events and the formulation of predictions based on the observation of such events.

Now if something is the violation of such a law, we should have to say that it is an irregular occurrence of a counter-instance of such events. Indeed, that the violation is irregular only will not do. In order for it to be a genuine counter-instance it will have to be non-repeatable, since its repetition would accord it (at least) some degree of regularity and thus would allow description as a repeatable, and possibly predictable, phenomenon. But if the violation occurs unpredictably and is not repeatable its occurrence could only then be describable in terms of natural laws and hence properly called a violation.

Again, Holland tells the story of a horse, deprived of nourishment (of which fact we can be certain) yet goes on thriving:

'A series of thorough examinations reveals no abnormality in the horse's condition... This is utterly inconsistent with our whole conception of the needs and capacities of horses; and because it is an impossibility in the light of our prevailing conception, my objector, in the event of its happening would expect us to abandon the conception – as though we had to have consistency at any price. Whereas the position I advocate is that the price is too high and it would be better to be left with inconsistency; and that in any event the prevailing conception has a logical status not altogether unlike that of a necessary truth and cannot be simply thrown away as a mistake – not when it rests on the experience of generations, not when all the other horses in the world are continuing to behave as horses have always done, and especially not when one considers the way our conception of the needs and capacities of horses interlocks with conceptions of the needs and capacities of other living things and with the conception of the difference between animate and inanimate behaviour quite generally. These conceptions form part of a common understanding that is well-established and is with us to stay.'[2]

Holland cannot mean what he says when he writes 'the prevailing conception has a logical status not altogether unlike that of a necessary truth' because if this conception includes natural laws, and from his example this is definitely so, then Holland must construe these laws as 'not unlike necessary truths' which will count decisively against his thesis that a possible counter-instance or violation of such laws might occur.

From this example and two others (one of levitation, and one of 'water into wine') Holland concludes:

'My thesis then in regard to the violation concept of the miraculous... is that a conflict of certainties is a necessary though not a sufficient condition of the miraculous. In other words, a miracle, though it cannot only be this, must at least be something the occurrence of which can be categorised at one and the same time as empirically certain and conceptually impossible. If it were less than conceptually impossible it would reduce to merely a very unusual occurrence such as could be treated (because of the empirical certainty) in the manner of a decisive experiment and result in a modification of the prevailing conception of natural law; while if it were less than empirically certain nothing more would be called for in regard to it than a suspension of judgement. So if there is to be a type of the miraculous other than the coincidence, it must offend against the principle *ab esse ad posse valet consequentia* [whatever is the case can be the case]. And since the violation concept of the miraculous does seem to me to be a possible concept I therefore reject that time-honoured logical principle.'[3]

Holland is making allowance for more than one kind of conceptual impossibility in this passage. What we have here is a case of contradiction with our 'common understanding' and 'the experience of generations'. He is pointing to such a thing as 'making sense, and failing to make sense, of events.' He is arguing that it is possible (conceptually? empirically?) that the conceptually impossible might occur. Now it may seem on the face of it that this is a *non sequitur*, but we shall see that this is not the case if we realise that Holland is vacillating between two different senses of 'conceptually impossible'. It is obvious that 'conceptually impossible' in this story does not amount to self-contradiction and hence is weaker than 'logically impossible'. What then is this weaker sense? Is there one? If one accepts Holland's argument about the certainty of empirical knowledge (in this case, of horses) based on the 'experience of generations' and that this, in some way or other, limits the possibilities of what we may or may not conceive, then his weaker notion of 'conceptually impossible' may be accorded sense. It seems that the 'experience of generations' in this case (and those of levitation and water-into-wine) refers basically to the findings of science. On Holland's view, any radical change of scientific theory which could be counted as sufficient to account for such events is impossible (conceptually? empirically?). While it may be maintained that such a change is possible (in whatever sense of 'possible' you like) Holland's findings will then be less than decisive and, at most, contradictory. I cannot see why such a change is either conceptually or empirically impossible and Holland provides no reason to substantiate his claim that this is so.

Antony Flew, although taking a similar line to Holland, arrives at his conclusions by a somewhat different method. Flew argues that a 'violation of the laws of nature' when used by Hume, means 'physically impossible event':

'The impossibility involved is not logical but physical. This physical impossibility of miraculous events is a consequence of the definition of the word "miracle". For "a miracle may be accurately defined" as "the transgression of the law of nature by a particular volition of the deity, or by the interposition of some invisible agent". And the criterion of physical as opposed to logical impossibility simply is logical incompatibility with a law of nature, in its broadest sense... It is an essential characteristic of all contingent, nomological propositions... that they imply the physical impossibility of any events with the occurrence of which they are inconsistent.'[4]

So for Flew an event is a miracle, in Hume's sense, if the statement of the event's occurrence is logically incompatible with the statement of the laws of nature; this is so because the laws of nature determine the limits of physical possibility, *ergo*, 'violation' signifies that which is physically impossible.

However, Flew's conception of 'violation' is not as straightforward as one might at first think. He says:

'The expression law of nature is sometimes taken as the prerogative of science. Whereas the notion of physical or empirical impossibility is quite untechnical, and surely antedates the emergence of science proper. It is an essential characteristic of all contingent nomological propositions, and not just members of the subclass which scientists are prepared to dignify with a diploma title laws of nature, that they imply the physical impossibility of any events with the occurrence of which they are inconsistent. It is only and precisely our knowledge, or presumed knowledge, of such nomological propositions which enables us to make the ordinary lay distinction between immensely improbable and sheerly impossible.'[5]

If we take the most commonly mentioned example of a law of nature, viz, the law of gravity, we might be able to clarify things somewhat. In our world, in which the law of gravity applies, and given the condition that no other forces present, any two objects will exert forces of attraction on each other which are proportional to the product of their masses and inversely proportional to the square of the distance between. Since a condition of our law is that no other forces are present, we should say that a violation of this law, in our world, would be when the two objects did not exert a force whereby they were attracted, e.g., if there was no attraction, or, if there were repulsion. These latter possibilities depict logically possible worlds, but in our world, they are physically impossible thus, by Flew's definition, would be miraculous.

How can we explain supernatural intervention except by reference to supernatural agents? If one is going to speak of miracles as 'supernatural volition' or 'the interposition of some invisible agent' then the idea of miracles in terms of violations can be explained only by reference to supernatural forces rather than to what is or is not logically inconsistent with the laws of nature.

Now while this might solve some problems it creates others. The only criterion by which a 'violation' miracle can be identified is the fact that it is a violation. But the concept of violations, if it is to be coherent, must have a 'supernatural precondition' built into it; this means that violation miracles can only be characterised on the precondition that they may be the result of a supernatural force at work, and that the activity of supernatural forces in relation to the violation concept of the miraculous can only be characterised in relation to the violations themselves. This is obviously circular. Or, to put it a little more technically: what determines the bounds of physical possibility is the counterfactual conditional relating to the fact that the objects will be attracted with a force determined by the product of the masses and the square of the distance between. Because it is specified that no other relevant forces are present, the only physical possibility in our world is the attraction of the objects in the way specified by an equation that expresses the relations of mass, distance, etc. But at once we encounter a difficulty in regard to the nature of 'other relevant forces' that may be present in a given situation. Are these forces 'the volition of the deity', or '... the interposition of some invisible agent' as Hume suggests, or are they 'natural' forces? The specification of natural or supernatural forces at work in this context will be a precondition that must accompany the counterfactual in the case of any purported violation. But this causes distinct ambiguities. One is that, if Hume's precondition is accepted, it becomes a supporting premise for a conclusion entailing false counterfactuals about what would happen in the absence of natural forces. For example, suppose that in our actual world there are no other natural forces present but there is a supernatural force counteracting the force of gravity in relation to two given objects such that the objects, which should be accelerating towards each other, in fact do not. The counterfactual conditional regarding the accelerated movement of objects on the precondition that there are no other natural forces present is fulfilled. Hence, we have here an instance of a physical impossibility and hence a miracle. But this means that the law of nature is false. It is false because it supports false counterfactuals about what would happen when no other natural forces are present, i.e. given that no other natural forces are present, there should have been accelerated motion of the two objects towards each other, whereas, in fact, there was not. In the case of a miracle, however, such a counterfactual is false; it begs the question of supernatural forces. Thus, the specification of forces present cannot be either/or (exclusive), it must be either/or (inclusive). The precondition must be that there are no other natural *or* supernatural forces present and not simply, as is the case in the scientific paradigm, that there are no other natural forces present. In this case, the law of gravity supports a counterfactual which states the acceleration of bodies towards each other unless *any* other force is present. Now, if this is correct, Flew's conception of physically impossible events becomes incoherent because if the presence of *any* (natural or supernatural) force is presupposed for any conditional entailed by a law, in what sense then can an event generally falling within the limits of the statement of that law be impossible?

Another problem has to do with how one could possibly identify a supernatural force at work (even in a violation) as opposed to natural forces; especially if it was a natural force unknown to science.

The whole concept of violation miracles is confused. Even if it were to make sense, it can in no way form the foundation of any sort of religious apology because if it is to be at all consistent it can only be characterised in terms of the operation of supernatural forces and not only by reference to logical inconsistency with the laws of nature. If this is the case, then any apology which endeavoured to demonstrate the existence of supernatural forces by means of the violation concept of the miraculous would have to assume the very existence of that which was the object of proof in order to maintain consistency in the proof itself; the argument would, necessarily, be circular.

Both notions of the miraculous are, therefore, incoherent.

We have seen how both Lessing and Kierkegaard grapple with the issue of the relationship of the disciple to the events that evince that discipleship. In so doing, they appear to accept the coherence of the notion of the miraculous. Even Hume appears to do the same. If I am right, however, the very incoherence of the concept of the miraculous renders their ruminations pointless. In that respect, we might wish to side with Kierkegaard in rejecting the need for Hegelian objectivity and make that passionate choice, that leap into faith.

Notes:

1. pp. 156-157, 'The Miraculous' in *Religion and Understanding*, (ed.) DZ Phillips, Blackwell, 1967.

2. *op. cit.*, pp. 165-166.
3. *op. cit.*, p. 167.
4. pp. 186-187, *Hume's Philosophy of Belief*, R & KP, 1961. Flew is quoting here from Hume's essay 'Of Miracles'.
5. *loc. cit.*

15

The Impotence of Agnosticism

Of all forms of unbelief, agnosticism is the most vulnerable, grounded as it is on there being insufficient evidence to know that there is, or is not, a God or gods. Agnosticism *eo ipso* is predicated on the deployment of evidence. As we shall see below, this belief is untenable. Moreover, holding religious belief to be propositional in nature can have unexpected adverse consequences for those who do so.

Agnosticism (Greek: not – know – ism). Unless this is an expression of dumb ignorance, it must entail a minimal propositional element. Modern day agnosticism is predicated on the misconception that belief is essentially propositional; that it is evidence-based. In particular: that there is insufficient evidence to show that God exists or does not exist.

I shall not engage in the current debate about just what it *means* to be an agnostic: we are told that 'strong' agnosticism is 'the conviction that nothing is known or can be known of immaterial things, especially with regards to the existence or nature of God' and 'weak' agnosticism is a 'lack of commitment or conviction which… may apply to one's attitude towards religious belief'[1] which may, or may not, approximate Huxley's 'metaphysical unknowing'. Then there is 'cancellation' agnosticism and 'sceptical' agnosticism, and so on. Then we need definitions of what 'convictions', 'immaterial', 'existence', 'commitment' and 'religious belief' are in order to understand the definitions of the definitions. Life is too short.

Blaise Pascal was born in 1632 in the Auvergne; he was a child prodigy, educated by his father at home with his sisters. At the age of ten, he started work on building mechanical calculators, some of which still exist. By 16, he worked on projective geometry and, later, corresponded with Fermat, working on probability or what today would be called Game Theory. Their specific interest was a problem of two players who want to finish a game early and, given the current circumstances of the game, want to divide the stakes fairly, based on the chance each has of winning the game at that point; a sort of Duckworth – Lewis solution for cricket interrupted by rain. Pascal's work had an influence on Leibniz's formulation of the calculus. He is famous for Pascal's Triangle, a convenient presentation for binomial coefficients. Pascal also worked on hydraulic fluids, in particular on hydrodynamics and hydrostatics; he invented the hydraulic press and the syringe.

In theology, he is best known for *Lettres provinciales, Pensees* and, popularly, for his *Wager*.

He died in 1662, two months after his 39th birthday. Pascal was condemned by Pope Innocent X in 1653.

The Wager, in brief, is this:

1) either God exists or he does not;
2) if God exists then the man who believes in him wins everything;
3) while, if God does not exist, the man who believes in him suffers only a finite loss.

The Wager is designed to show that there is an advantage in belief in God that is not available in not believing in God. But for agnostics, amongst others, there is a disadvantage in not believing because of the very nature of some forms of unbelief.

Agnosticism may take two forms: first, the claim that religious belief does not make sense for one; not that it is, in principle, incomprehensible, but that it simply means nothing to one particular individual. Now this might be the result of uninterest, and here will amount to saying, 'It just doesn't move me', or 'I don't care', or it may be the result of the fact that the enquirer simply cannot make anything of religious talk. So, to the proposition, 'God loves mankind', she might reply, 'I'm sorry, I just don't understand what that means; it means nothing whatsoever to me.'

This form of agnosticism does not suffer the

difficulties of its second manifestation for it entails no epistemic claims whatever and, as a consequence, cannot be accused of the kind of linguistic duplicity I shall argue is involved in the second form. The central issue here is that the agnostic does not claim to understand a notion she then rejects as untenable. She claims not to understand the notion at all. I can see nothing incoherent in this although, as we shall see when we consider Flew's 'negative atheism', it is not without its problems.

The second form of agnosticism is the belief that we do not have sufficient evidence to know that there is, or is not, a God.

Some will be familiar with the argument that God's existence is necessary. The Ontological Argument takes many and varied forms and generally contains a premise to the effect that our conception of God, or God's nature, entails necessary existence. For example, Norman Malcolm has argued for the validity of Anselm's second ontological proof, which is not simply that God is *aliquid quo nihil maius cogitari possit*, a greater than which cannot be conceived, but that 'a being whose nonexistence is logically impossible is "greater" than a being whose nonexistence is logically possible (and therefore that a being greater than which cannot be conceived must be one whose nonexistence is logically impossible)'[2]. This extends the claim that existence is a perfection, which is generally thought to be false, to the claim that necessary existence is a perfection, which Malcolm argues is true. In other words, God's existence is not contingent.

While many will accept that the *concept* of God requires necessary existence, some persist in asking whether there is *in fact* a God who so exists. But, according to Malcolm, to ask whether in fact there is such a being depends on the possibility of regarding the subject as something which may or may not exist; and this is a self-contradictory position to maintain. At one and the same time, the person who wishes to pursue this course of reason has said:

1) God's nonexistence is logically impossible, or, that God's existence is necessary existence, and,
2) God might not exist,

which entails that his existence is contingent : (2) contradicts (1).

Some have argued that this misses the point; that the necessity of the existence of God reflects merely our use of words and does not refer to the facts. Such an argument was made by JN Findlay who thought that the view that logical necessity 'reflects our use of words' implies, not that nothing has necessary properties, but that existence cannot be a necessary property of anything. That is to say, every proposition of the form 'x exists', including the proposition 'God exists', must be contingent. At the same time, our concept of God requires that his existence be necessary, that is, that 'God exists' be a necessary truth. Therefore, the modern view of necessity proves that what the concept of God requires cannot be fulfilled. It proves that God cannot exist.

Malcolm's answer to Findlay's argument is: 'The correct reply is that the view that logical necessity merely reflects the use of words cannot possibly have the implication that every existential statement must be contingent. That requires us to look at the use of words and not manufacture *a priori* theses about it. In the Ninetieth Psalm it is said: "Before the mountains were brought forth, or ever thou hast formed the earth and the world, even from everlasting to everlasting, thou art God." Here is expressed the idea of the necessary existence and eternity of God, an idea that is essential to the Jewish and Christian religions. In those complex systems of thought, those "language games", God has the status of a necessary being. Here we must say with Wittgenstein, "This language game is played".'[3]

If the agnostic wants to say that we do not have sufficient reason to know that there is, or is not, a God then this entails that she knows what it is for a being to be God. If I say, 'We do not have sufficient reason to believe that there are, or are not, fairies' then this means that I do not believe there is adequate evidence for the existence of beings that are, say, approximately six inches tall, are equipped with wings, and who live at the bottom of my garden. It makes no sense to affirm or to deny the existence of something about which one knows nothing or which one comprehends not. In other words, the agnostic is questioning the grounds to support the existence of a certain being which has *certain properties predicated of it*. Now if she claims to comprehend the concept of God she may find herself in some distinct difficulties. Will she side with the school of thought, of which Findlay was once one (he later withdrew his argument), which holds that God's non-existence is logically impossible, or that the concept of God requires necessary existence? If so, and I suggest she should, she will become embroiled in the debate above, i.e. whether a belief that God's non-existence is logically impossible is inconsistent with the belief that God might not exist. We should take such a construal to be an unwitting attempt on the part of the agnostic of denying the principle of non-contradiction, i.e.:

1) if God exists, then his existence is necessary,
2) God might not exist.

(1) is incompatible with (2) because if God's existence is necessary then it is not possible that he might not exist (not both p and not p). This latter belief, that God might not exist, is surely a minimum thesis of agnosticism.

If, on the other hand, she sides with the other camp and does not construe God's non-existence as logically impossible, it is hard to see how this belief amounts to little more than atheism. A view which asserts the contingency of God's existence is compatible with those held by, say, Sartre or Nietzsche. For Sartre, *'Dieu n'existe pas'*, he says, 'He is dead, he spoke to us and is now silent...' And, in *The Gay Science*, Nietzsche (following the poet Swinburne before him) tells the parable of the madman announcing the death of God in the marketplace and entering the churches of the realm to sing a *requiem aeternam deo* of the God who once was, but now is slain. That, surely, is the whole force of saying that God's existence is contingent; it means that God might cease to exist. Yet when Sartre and Nietzsche affirm the logical consequence of the contingency concept of God's existence they are not being agnostics, but atheists. To say 'God is dead' is the same, materially, as saying 'There is no God'. It can also be argued that it is the same, logically, as saying 'God might not exist'. It will not do to claim that the difference between the atheist and agnostic in this respect is simply that the one, the atheist, claims that God is dead while the other, the agnostic, holds a view which entails the possibility of God's death. This, after all, is an argument about the nature of God. It is clear that both Sartre and Nietzsche construe God's death as the work of man. This is an argument which can be enjoined by anyone who philosophises; one can argue about whether God's existence is necessary or contingent without being a committed atheist, theist, or agnostic. So what makes the agnostic different from the atheist in this respect?

Agnosticism in the sense we are talking about is the belief that we do not have sufficient reason either to affirm or to deny God's existence. Presumably the sufficient reason, among other things, applies to the linguistic reasons about the nature of the concept of God. And therefore, the agnostic must remain agnostic about linguistic arguments. If this does not mean that the agnostic must be irrational over one area of linguistic debate (which I take it it does not mean), it does mean that she might find it difficult to be committed to a view ('there is not sufficient reason to know that...') which requires non-commitment ('neither God is nor is not...') and yet to which, if she is to claim to understand the view about which she is uncommitted then there must be, at least, some level of commitment (i.e. if God is, He is this, rather than that...).

(Frege draws a distinction between first-level and second-level concept expressions. Concept expressions of the first-level are those which require completion with the name (or singular term) to yield a grammatical sentence. Those of the second-level require completion by a first-level concept expression to yield a grammatical sentence. There is no difficulty in identifying predicates with Frege's first-level concept expressions. 'Exists', however, has a strong claim to membership of the second-level. One consequence of this is that once a Descriptivist Theory of Names is abandoned it is no longer possible to treat positive and negative existentials as about concepts – as say, of a particular concept, that it is or is not uniquely instantiated. Accordingly, 'exists', can no longer be treated as a second-level predicate requiring completion by first-level predicate; it must be seen as on a par logically with ordinary first-level predicates, requiring completion by a singular term to form a sentence. This, besides raising difficulties such as those surrounding the possibility of a valid ontological argument for the existence of God, widens the gap between quantificational logic and the ordinary language sentences it is intended to symbolise.)

We might restate our precursor to the *Wager* as follows:

1) if God exists then his existence is necessary (because if it were possible that he might not exist then he would not be God).
2) If a person believes God's existence is necessary and yet believes that God might not exist then she is maintaining a view which is self-contradictory (both p not p).

We have seen that one form of agnosticism at least amounts to this view. Therefore, one form of agnosticism, at least, is self-contradictory.

But suppose that I'm wrong about to above. Suppose it is possible to maintain both:

a) that God's nonexistence is logically impossible (i.e. that His existence is necessary) and,
b) that God might not exist.

At this point I'm not really interested in how this might be possible but one can imagine various arguments, say, that (a) is a notion which relates to propositions only, whereas (b) is an existential proposition. Whatever the reason may be, however, suppose that it is possible to maintain both (a) and (b) without contradiction. I suggest that the agnostic, in asserting (b) is espousing a view which amounts to little less than atheism.

A minimum requirement of atheism is that it is possible that God might not exist, which is entailed by 'God does not exist'. Both these propositions could be regarded as, respectively, the necessary and sufficient conditions of atheism (note here that old principle of modal logic: *ab esse ad posse valet consequentia* – whatever is the case can be the case). God does not exist, therefore it is possible that God does not exist. This minimum requirement atheism (it is possible that God does not exist), is a simple statement of the contingency concept of God's existence embodied in (b) which is, in turn, a sufficient condition of at least one form of agnosticism. Therefore, one form of agnosticism is equivalent to a minimal requirement of atheism.

How does this relate to the *Wager*? The answer is quite simple: the argument I have presented is largely about what is believed, i.e. the things believed by theists (that God's existence is necessary), by agnostics (that God might not exist) and by atheists (that God does not or could not, exist). The *Wager*, on the other hand, is largely about the advantages or disadvantages of certain sorts of belief, i.e. if one believes that God exists then one stands to gain more than if one believes that God does not exist. While the *Wager* is designed to show that there is advantage in belief, I have shown that there is disadvantage in certain forms of unbelief. My contention, and the *Wager*, do not amount to the same thing because even if there is disadvantage in certain forms of disbelief or unbelief this does not mean that there is therefore advantage in certain forms of belief. Such a conclusion would be a simple logical error. I have tried to show that there is a certain inconsistency in one form of agnosticism and that this same difficulty, as we shall see later, also applies to atheism.

The agnostic gains no advantage in maintaining the sort of belief we have been examining for several reasons: one is the simple reason that it is undesirable to contradict oneself. The second has to do with a general observation that I have often heard expressed. It is that agnosticism is, somehow or other, more 'intellectually respectable' than atheism; that the agnostic is 'keeping her options open' in that, unlike the atheist, she is not committed to a view which may prove false. In short, agnosticism is sometimes construed to be a detached, uncommitted view. This general presumption is false. Not only may agnosticism be more closely allied to atheism than is sometimes assumed, it may also, at least in the form I have considered it, be wrong. There can be no 'intellectual respectability' attaching to a view which is wrong.

Notes:

1. p. 5, *Agnosticism*, ed. Hyman and Fallon, OUP, 2020.
2. 'Anselm's Ontological Arguments', *Philosophical Review,* lxix, 1960.
3. *ibid.,* pp. 55-56.

16
Four Types of (Un)belief

Insofar as atheism is propositional, it too must address the issues facing agnosticism covered in chapter 15.

Atheism

Atheism: (a – theism) means literally 'not-Godism' and is the belief that there is no God of any kind. This may take various forms: it might be that one thinks it makes sense to say there is a God, whereas there is no God. Alternatively, one might believe that talk of God is meaningless. Atheism may rest on either of the following:

Scepticism - the ancestor of modern-day scepticism is, for many, David Hume. Hume employs reason to demonstrate the limitations of reason. The 'idea of a substance... is nothing but a collection of simple ideas, that are united by the imagination, and have a particular name assigned to them, by which we are able to recall, either to ourselves or to others, that collection' (*Treatise* I.i.6). Thus knowledge is limited to sense-data and perception of anything beyond, because of this limitation, is not possible. Hume's famous denial of causation led him to believe that all that we are in the habit of thinking of as cause and effect is really a matter of sequence; a habit of mind. We know nothing of the external world but impressions and copies of impressions between which we can discover only succession, but not necessary connection. Causation is thus only a subjective belief maintained by memory and explanation. But this makes for problems. On what foundation is Hume going to insist on the distinction between truths of reason and matters of fact? It seems that the sceptic is not quite sceptical enough. Since it is assumed that there is no necessary connection between states of mind, no persistence of the self from moment to moment, it is not possible to be sure that the conclusions of an argument follow from the supposed premises. It is only by lack of courage that the sceptic saves nature and history, indeed, the world about him, from the flames to which he commits the Divinity.

Theological doubt and anti-theism - we may group these two together because they suffer similar difficulties. Both make epistemic claims and so, in this respect, resemble agnosticism. The theological doubter, unlike the agnostic, thinks that there are good reasons to incline her to disbelieve the claims of theism. These reasons might not be conclusive, but they are enough to engender doubt; but doubt about what? In this respect, the atheist's belief must be propositional.

There are, today, interminable arguments about seemingly endless definitions of atheism: there are 'soft' or 'weak' atheists and 'strong' atheists; there are 'old' atheists and 'New Atheists' (Richard Dawkins, Sam Harris, Christopher Hitchens and Daniel Dennett – sometimes known as 'The Four Horsemen'), and so on. On the principle that calculating the number of angels on the head of a pin is not a worthwhile exercise, I shall not trawl through the seemingly endless variety of definitions of atheism which, at times, detract from the actual issue at hand.

Antony Flew (1923-2010) was, until his conversion to Deism towards the end of his life, 'the world's most notorious atheist'. Flew retired as Professor of Philosophy at Reading University in 1983. He was much-published and, in 1972, wrote an article *The Presumption of Atheism*[1] in which he argued in favour of 'negative atheism'. The negative atheist is 'someone who is not a theist' and on an analogy with the English Common Law principle that someone is innocent until proven guilty, he contended, as Shelley had before him, that the onus of proof lies with the theist, just as the onus of proof, in law, lies with the prosecution.

Flew's paper provoked a storm of comment, as did an earlier article, *Theology and Falsification*, written in 1950 when he was an undergraduate at Oxford. But, according to his long-time antagonist W.L. Craig, his 'presumption' (which later was called 'weak' or 'soft' atheism) became 'one of the most commonly proffered justifications of atheism'. Towards the end of his life, it appears he adopted the God of Aristotle[2] based on, of all things, a version of the Design Argument. Much unseemly controversy followed in attempts by atheists and, bizarrely, evangelical Christians to claim an increasingly demented Flew as their own.

Flew's characterisation of an atheist as anyone who is not a theist is not without problems: on this basis, the demented, the newborn and gorillas are all atheists. To overcome this difficulty, one has to qualify this atheistical lack of belief by a cognitive awareness of such a lack. But the addition of such a qualification makes it difficult to see how such a position is significantly different from Flew's 'positive atheist': someone who believes there is no God.

It is also difficult to see what thesis one is supporting when one does not deny that God exists but simply lacks a belief in God. What, for example, of those who argue that all propositions containing the term 'God' are neither true nor false precisely because they are unintelligible or conceptually incoherent, as does the Logical Positivist A.J. Ayer:

'To say that "God exists" is to make a metaphysical utterance which cannot be either true or false. And by the same criterion, no sentence which purports to describe the nature of a transcendent God can possess any literal significance.

'It is important not to confuse this view of religious assertions with the view that is adopted by atheists, or agnostics. For it is characteristic of an agnostic to hold that the existence of a God is a possibility in which there is no good reason either to believe or disbelieve; and it is characteristic of an atheist to hold that it is at least probable that no God exists. And our view that all utterances about the nature of God are nonsensical, so far from being identical with, or even lending any support to, either of these familiar contentions, is actually incompatible with them. For if the assertion that there is a God is nonsensical, then the atheist's assertion that there is no God is equally nonsensical, since it is only a significant proposition that can be significantly contradicted.'[3]

Is this a non-cognitivist version of negative atheism and how does it differ from positive atheism? For this conceptually incoherent God must have at least some properties predicated of him if the term 'God' is to refer.

There is also the problem for Flew that a valid proof of the existence of God, he says, will scupper his contention of negative atheism. Alvin Plantinga offers one such proof in his reworking of Anselm's Second Ontological Argument. In essence, and only that, Plantinga's proof is:

> 1. a being has maximal excellence in a given

possible world W if and only if it is omnipotent, omniscient and wholly good in W, and

2. a being has maximal greatness if it has maximal excellence in every possible world.
3. It is possible that there is a being that has maximal greatness.
4. Therefore, possibly, it is necessarily true that an omnipotent, omniscient, wholly good being exists.
5. Therefore, it is necessarily true that an omnipotent, omniscient, wholly good being exists.
6. Therefore, an omnipotent, omniscient and wholly good being exists.

Given that this is valid, as the *Oxford Companion to Philosophy* says its full version is, then is Flew scuppered? But consider here the absurdity of stumbling across Plantinga's argument and thinking: 'Oh, that's valid. I'd better be a believer now'. This sort of response bears no relation to faith and underscores the nonsense of regarding faith as propositional belief.

Either way, Flew's argument fails: negative atheism is not agnosticism because the agnostic thinks it makes sense to say there is a God. Anthony Kenny shows the difficulty for the negative atheist:

'I think it is correct to say that there is a presumption in favour of ignorance over knowledge: that is to say, it takes more effort to show that you do know something than it takes to show that you don't know something. But I do not know why one should call the position of ignorance – the position of not knowing whether there is a God, perhaps not knowing whether it even makes sense to say there is one – negative atheism. One could just as well have divided the field in the following way: a positive theist is someone who positively accepts the existence of God, and a negative theist is simply somebody who is not an atheist. In that case, by a simple redefinition, all Flew's arguments would establish a presumption of theism rather than a presumption of atheism – a presumption of negative theism, of course, but then, after all, it was only a presumption of negative atheism which he claimed to establish himself.'[4]

Kenny goes on to contend that, given the acceptance of the notion of God as a coherent concept, then the negative theist and the negative atheist are both better called agnostics.

Atheism is, inevitably, a negative thing, defined by what it is not. More often than not, atheism is critical of what religion is not; it mistakes its target. I shall investigate four different ways of looking at the world, four different epistemologies which have implications for belief and unbelief. I don't claim to prove the truth of any one, much less even to resolve the differences between them. My aim is to present the reader with an overview of differing, even competing, ways of looking at how we know and thus to attempt to identify something of the anatomy of belief and unbelief.

Like falling out of love, the growth of belief or unbelief is rarely sudden – an epiphany of the awareness of error or stupidity or whatever. The seeds of unbelief and belief are sown in a burgeoning understanding of the nature of things, a gradual enlightenment.

1. The God Hypothesis

In his pamphlet, *The Necessity of Atheism*, Percy Bysshe Shelley (1792-1822) says: 'God is an hypothesis, and, as such, stands in need of proof: the *onus probandi* rests on the theist'. Hume reminds us that: 'a wise man proportions his belief according to the evidence' and Locke warns us about 'not entertaining any proposition with greater assurance than the proofs it is built upon will warrant'.

Essentially, any attempt to infer the existence of God from the world about us and to employ the notion of evidence in support of such inferences is to treat God's existence as a hypothesis. Most unbelievers construe religion in this way. As we shall see below, whether God exists, or not, is a trivial question.

A particularly influential philosopher who perpetuated the God hypothesis myth is David Hume. Hume (1711 – 76) was a Scottish philosopher, essayist and historian. He was known, during his lifetime, as the 'Great Infidel'. Hume was the progenitor of modern empiricism.

Although born into a minor noble Scottish family in Edinburgh, his father's early death meant he had largely to fend for himself. At a young age, he studied philosophy and literature at Edinburgh University and then, after a brief interlude pursuing the law and later clerking in Bristol, he went to La Fleche in Anjou (1734 – 7), the town where, 100 years before, Descartes had studied. Here he wrote *Treatise on Human Nature*. The work was, at first, not well-received. But later, it was held in high esteem, particularly by twentieth-century empiricists.

The *Treatise* – his most widely-studied text today – was subtitled *An Attempt to introduce the experimental method of reasoning into Moral Subjects*. He had more initial success in 1741/2 with two volumes of *Essays: Moral and Political*.

After failing to be appointed to the chair of Ethics and Pneumatical Philosophy in Edinburgh, he became tutor to a mad nobleman and then secretary to Gen. St Clair who led an abortive attempt to invade France.

Hume reworked the *Treatise* into *Philosophical Essays Concerning Human Understanding* (1748) to include his chapter *Of Miracles*. The second edition appeared in 1751, bearing the title we now know it by: *An Enquiry Concerning Human Understanding*. Later, he produced *Dialogues Concerning Natural Religion* (1751), though because of its incendiary nature he suppressed it until just after his death. In his will, Hume asked his friend, Adam Smith the economist, to arrange for its publication. Smith refused, so it was left to Hume's nephew to do so. It finally appeared in 1779, gaining immediate success and notoriety. It remains one of the classic texts in discussions about the nature of the evidence presented to prove the existence of God and the character of his attributes.

While working as librarian to the Faculty of Advocates in Edinburgh, Hume wrote a *History of England* which was a great success.

After a short spell in Paris (1763-6) where he met Rousseau and was the darling of the philosophical salons, he returned to London as under-secretary of state in the Northern Department.

Hume returned to Edinburgh in 1769 and there he died, probably of bowel cancer, in 1776.

It is difficult to categorise Hume's religious stance: is he an atheist, an agnostic or a theist? He denied the validity of metaphysical arguments for God's existence; he treats the Argument from Design as leading to a 'religious hypothesis'. And in the *Dialogues,* he makes clear his unhappiness with any argument from analogy of human constructions to the construction of the world. Anthony Kenny tells us: ' ... he was an agnostic, not an atheist' but he 'enjoyed annoying the clergy and ... he detested Christianity itself'. Kenny says: '...Hume made a lasting, if negative, contribution to natural theology. His critical observations on the arguments for the existence of God, and his discussion of the role of miracles in establishing the authority of a revelation, have remained points of departure for both theist and atheist philosophers of religion.'[5]

In the *Dialogues*, patterned after Cicero's *De Natura Deorum*, there are three characters: Cleanthes, Philo and Demea. While Demea is ruled out of contention, there is debate about which of the others represents Hume's own views.

In Part 1, Cleanthes presents the Argument from Design: the information and evidence we have about the natural world enables us to infer both the existence and nature of a deity. This argument became extremely popular in the form given it by Sir Isaac Newton. Look at the world, says Cleanthes, and you will see that it is nothing but one vast machine, subdivided into smaller machines. All of the parts are adjusted to one another, so that the whole complex functions harmoniously. The adaptation of means to ends through all of nature exactly resembles the adaptation which results from human design and intelligence. Since natural objects and human artefacts resemble one another, we infer by analogy, that the causes of them must also resemble one another. Hence, the author of nature must be similar to the mind of man, though he must have greater faculties, since his production is greater.

Probably speaking through the character of Philo, Hume laid the groundwork for a reductionism which has been evident in the work of empiricists, and indeed philosophers of religion, ever since. DZ Phillips notes three levels of argument of increasing severity in the *Dialogues* based on Hume's assumption that belief in religion is founded on inferences from the world about us to the existence of God. In considering the Argument from Design we find that the first level 'depends on the fact that there is a fundamental ambiguity both in the evidence offered and in the character of the author to be inferred from the evidence'[6]. Essentially, this has to do with the appropriateness of the inferences made: one cannot infer a God whose nature is perfect, etc. from the chaotic world he is supposed to have created. The problem here is that no matter how ambiguous the character of the evidence from which God's existence is inferred, it is still employing the notion of evidence; but the existence of God, says Phillips, cannot be settled by appealing to the evidence.

Secondly, Hume calls into question the appropriateness of talking about design in nature at all: to speak of planning or design as a feature of nature is already to be highly selective. Once we do treat nature naturally, the analogy between natural phenomena and human artefacts collapses[7].

Thirdly, and with particular reference to the Cosmological Argument (which attempts to prove God's existence from the fact that things exist), Philo asks whether one can ask questions about everything in the way one can ask questions about particular things. Hume is asking 'whether it makes sense to ask questions about the origin of the universe, and he is denying that an analogy with questions about the origin of particular things will bring any sense to such questions': there are important differences in asking how some artefact came to be and how the universe came to be. But we need not here rehearse the failure of classical arguments for God's existence. Phillips concludes: 'The effect of these levels of argument which go to make up Hume's legacy is to make any attempt to infer the existence of God from the world in which we live logically problematic'[8].

Hume's arguments in this respect are deeply flawed: what he has to say about ideas is hardly consistent with what he says a cause is. As I shall argue, Hume assumes too much: religious beliefs are not inferences from the world about us to the existence of God. If this is so, then Hume's foundations crumble.

We have already encountered the work of Richard Swinburne. Swinburne is a successor of Hume. JL Mackie (1917 – 1981) was an Australian philosopher who, from 1967, was a fellow of University College, Oxford. Like Swinburne, Mackie was a fellow of the British Academy. Mackie, too, was a successor of Hume and considered that there is good evidence against religious belief, construed as a proposition that God exists:

'It is my view that the question whether there is or is not a God can and should be discussed rationally and reasonably, and that such discussions can be rewarding, in that it can yield definite results.'[9]

'Rationally and reasonably', for Mackie, involves taking descriptions of God fairly literally: 'It is sometimes doubted whether such descriptions can be literally meaningful. But there really is no problem about this...'[10] and the definite results that Mackie believes the discussion of whether there is a God or not will yield are, he says elsewhere, that:

'... it can be shown, not that religious beliefs lack rational support, but that they are positively irrational, that the several parts of the essential theological doctrine are inconsistent with one another, so that the theologian can maintain his position as a whole only by a much more extreme rejection of reason than in the former case. He must be prepared to believe, not merely what cannot be proved, but what can be *disproved* from other beliefs that he also holds'[11].

As we have seen, the notion of evidence is not unproblematical. For example, what is sufficient evidence? Mackie seems to be claiming that the maintenance of inconsistent beliefs constitutes sufficient evidence to disprove the hypothesis that God exists. So, if a believer believes that q and p support h, and q is inconsistent with p, then not h. But surely not. What about j and l and m which might support h and which bear no relation to q and p? The falsity of an argument does not entail the falsity of a conclusion except on the sole grounds of that argument, but not necessarily on other grounds.

Furthermore, it is not at all clear that having sufficient evidence for a false proposition is irrational, as Mackie seems to think. Was it really *irrational* for men to believe, prior to Copernicus and Galileo, that the earth is flat? They believed they had sufficient evidence.

Let us, however, overlook for the moment these other difficulties involved in the concept of evidence, and consider believing in God in relation to believing other propositions which might be thought to constitute evidence for it. But which are these other propositions? Would, for example, knowing a necessary proposition be relevant to, or evidence for, my belief in God? Or is it only contingent propositions? And how is it that we can be said to know necessary propositions and not to know that there is a God but only to believe in God? Certainly, I do not know necessary propositions in the way that I know contingent ones, so maybe there is a way of knowing appropriate to God which provides religion with its own rationality? I shall return to this question below.

What are we to say then of the thesis which construes religious belief as belief in propositions entailing probability-related evidence, of a kind encountered in Swinburne and Mackie, and often called a cognitivist form of faith or unfaith? First, we should note that there are some religious beliefs we have considered, e.g., historical claims (that Jesus rose from the dead – in some facets of the tradition), which are presented in the New Testament along cognitivist lines. These historical claims are corrigible, and believed to be so, but are presented with evidence which, it is believed, renders them probable. We have also seen that faith intends past events, therefore faith is, to that extent at least, cognitivist. On the other hand, we have found no evidence that the early church used empirical evidence to support metaphysical conclusions in the way that Swinburne and others wish to do. Faith is not a matter of assent to propositions when it is construed as propositional assent entailing probability-related evidence statements.

Both Mackie and Swinburne see the rather tedious debates between believer and unbeliever as debates between opposing hypotheses, the strength of which will be judged by the evidence adduced. But see how far this philosophical speculation is removed from the world of religious worship. A clear observation of religious belief and practice will reveal no indication whatsoever of the religious entertaining hypotheses, of them believing in the high probability that there is a God.

Look in the Bible for attempts to prove the existence of God. You will not find them. Look in the Bible for attempts to provide evidence of God's existence. You will not find them. How can this be if religious belief entails believing in a God who exists? In religious belief construed as propositional belief we are confronted by the anomaly that this method of identifying religious belief actually distorts its true character.

Given the success of Hume's enterprise, religion

can no longer be seen as inferences from the world about us to the existence of God. But what if religious belief is no such thing? What if religious belief is a purely natural phenomenon?

Others of Hume's reductionist successors have offered alternative senses for religious beliefs which result in an explanation that is, say, psychological or sociological. I'm thinking here of people like Marx ('it is the nature of a spiritual being to create itself by objectifying the world and then comprehending that world as its adequate expression'), Freud (the libido encompasses love for parents, children and humanity in general, thus religion seen as loving one's neighbour is to be understood through the prism of the libido and the idea of God turns out to be a version of the image of a human father), Durkheim (who attempted to provide functional explanations of religion: it is purely a social phenomenon serving the needs of the society in which it is practised, and the object of its cult, concealed under the figures of its particular mythology, is the society itself), Feuerbach (an extraordinary hostility to religion seen through the lens of his naturalistic humanism: man's ideas of God are projections of man's own wishes), and so on. Such attempts which see religious belief as really about one thing, despite the protestations of the believer, cannot be seen as explanations of what believers *do* believe so much as what academics seem to think believers *should* believe; they distinguish between what believers *think* they are doing and what *in fact* they are doing; by explaining religious belief thus they do away with the need for it.

For Freud, religion came about through murder: sons who murdered their fathers through envy of their sexual *droit de seigneur*, as seen in the Oedipus complex (of course, the irony is that the one person not suffering from an Oedipus complex was Oedipus himself. The Oedipus Complex is a Freudian fiction; it is not latent in the Theban plays of Sophocles. Oedipus unintentionally and unknowingly kills his father and marries, and has children by, his mother; he has no desire, conscious or sub-conscious, to do so. What he does is in fact the last thing on earth he would want to do and it is what he has unintentionally done that makes him cursed. In missing the point of Sophocles' plays, Freud has distorted the very dimension of guilt and remorse that makes the plays such morally challenging masterpieces). The father is seen as a rival in claims to the female's sexual favours. But regret ensures that in death the Father is more influential than he had been in life and the sons expiate their sin by making sacrifices to the dead Father's spirit's totem. Herein, so Freud, lies the origin of sacrifice to the gods.

Freud wants to add to this fanciful account a similar assessment of the elevation and consumption of the host during the Mass: the guilt occasioned by killing the father now sees the Father himself providing the sacrifice. But, in the consumption of the host, the original killing is re-enacted. Thus, at the end of *Totem and Taboo*, Freud wants, quoting Goethe, to change the opening words of John's Gospel: *In the beginning was the Word* (Greek*: logos*), to: *In the beginning was the Deed* (*Im anfang war die Tat*), meaning the father's murder by his sons. Historically, of course, this explanation is baseless. Moreover, it fails to account for the fact that the explanation of an origin may not account for an explanation of meaning. While it may not be a nonsense to suggest that God, as 'Father', is an analogue drawn from his earthly counterpart, it is no ground whatsoever for concluding that what one says of God can be explained only in terms of earthly fathers. Essentially, Freud is offering an alternative way of seeing God; he is not explaining what religious believers think when the Eucharist is said, he is offering a competing myth; it is pure aetiology, a figment of Freud's febrile imagination, although not without literary precedent, e.g. Kronos and Zeus. Freud fails to show that religious beliefs are mistaken (although he clearly saw himself as offering an explanation of – erroneous – religious belief), he simply offers an alternative myth. As Wittgenstein says:

'Freud refers to various ancient myths in these connections, and claims that his researches have now explained how it came about that anybody should think or propound a myth of a sort.

'Whereas in fact Freud has done something quite different. He has not given a scientific explanation of the ancient myth. What he has done is propound a new myth. The attractiveness of the suggestion, for instance, that all anxiety is repetition of the anxiety of the birth trauma, is just the attractiveness of a mythology. "It is all the outcome of something that happened long ago." Almost like referring to a totem.'[12]

In presenting religion this way, Freud is actually obscuring the real nature of belief. But notice the transition here: we have moved from inferences from the world to God, say in Hume's comments on the Design Argument, to an attempted demonstration that God is the product of human, in this case psychological, design. God becomes man's unwitting contrivance; a common reductionist theme.

Religious beliefs are not based on opinions or hypotheses. Rather they are themselves expressions of what is of value to the believer: they are not *founded* on mistaken hypotheses or inadequate evidence; they are not *founded* on anything; they are a way of seeing the world. Phillips offers an example:

'We accompany our dead to their graves. Does that practice rest on an opinion or an hypothesis?

It was once suggested that this was so. Accompanying the dead to their graves was the practical means of securing the imprisonment of the dead and that they would not return to haunt the living, hence the obliterating of the homeward path. But are there no other possibilities of understanding here? In accompanying the dead to their graves, why need one be expressing one's faith in any hypothesis? In walking to the grave, one may, in the language of gesture, be showing something about the meaning of life and death. We walk to the end with a loved one with whom we have walked in life. Is that any kind of hypothesis? His life is over and the hearth will see him no more. His footsteps will no longer come to the door, they have been obliterated from the face of the earth. Is that any kind of hypothesis? What we see in this ritual is an expression of an attitude to life and death.'[13]

There is, of course, a reason why these reductionists wish to account for religious beliefs in terms of mistaken hypotheses: they entertain the Enlightenment fantasy that man is enjoying the onward march of development from primaeval stupidity to cultivated sophistication and in so doing shedding the mistaken, mental detritus of the past. The same myth as peddled by de Chardin and so many others in thrall to the Enlightenment's nostrums. This doctrine of development is a chimera; if anything, we are very much more primitive now than we were in Voltaire's or Rousseau's or Hume's time.

Atheism, in this context, is like Mackie's: religious belief is a mistaken or improbable hypothesis. Insofar as religious belief is no such thing, this type of atheism is very wide of the mark. Indeed, it is mistaken.

John Gray, in *Seven Types of Atheism*[14] , considers those who attacked religion as if it were 'an obsolete scientific theory'. He identifies J.G. Frazer, author of *The Golden Bough, a Study in Magic and Religion*, August Comte, and Henri de Saint-Simon as 'new atheists'. Following Comte in particular, modern day new atheists regard religion as a primitive sort of science. Gray, quoting Wittgenstein on Frazer, is rightly dismissive of Richard Dawkins: '[he] is much more savage than most of his savages … His explanations of primitive practices are much cruder than the meaning of these practices themselves.'[15]

Frazer, according to Wittgenstein, suffered from the disease of a mania for explanation – something not uncommon in a culture where technology and scientific methodology play such an important role. Consequently, Frazer tries to explain a variety of religious phenomena and beliefs as just so many erroneous beliefs (explanatory hypotheses) which lead 'savages' in futile attempts to manipulate the world about them. Frazer's aim is to uncover the basis of belief upon which the mistaken magical practices are built. Wittgenstein, however, wants to say that there is an evocational and instinctive role in 'primitive' behaviour:

'When I am angry about something, I sometimes beat on the ground … with my stick. But I certainly don't believe that the earth is guilty or that beating it can help. "I give vent to my anger." All rites are like that. Such actions can be called instinctive. A historical explanation – that I or my ancestors at one time believed that my beating the earth would help – is illusory, for it … explains nothing. What is important is the similarity of the act with an act of punishment, but nothing more than this similarity is to be stated.'[16]

The magical rites of primitive society then are, according to Wittgenstein, analogous to the symbolic acts with which we are familiar in our own social behaviour. We might disabuse ourselves of the notion that behind magical practices and beliefs there lies some body of erroneous theory. Such beliefs could only be erroneous if truth-values could be accorded to them, i.e. if they are probability-related propositional beliefs. But insofar as rites and associated beliefs are not statements of opinion about certain states of affairs, or what is the case, etc., then truth-theory is inappropriate here. Both beliefs and rites may be symbols (one must beware here of the assumption that symbols are substitutes for reality – not all language is referential and not all referential language is non-symbolic) and to understand their meaning, as symbols, it will be necessary to see the whole network of interrelated symbols, beliefs, practices, etc., of which they are part. Thus there is a point where sense, understood in Fregean terms, is, in part, suspended.

To construe religious belief as a hypothesis is mistaken.

2. Foundationalism

In its classical formulation, Foundationalism is a variety of epistemology which is more often than not atheistical.

Foundationalism is the belief that knowledge of the world rests on given beliefs – what Wittgenstein calls 'bedrock' propositions – from which further propositions can be inferred to make up the corpus of known truths. So-called necessary truths (e.g. 2+2 = 4) and propositions expressing sensory experience (e.g. 'I see a tree'), what Russell and Ayer called sense-data, are typically foundational propositions which are usually called *basic* propositions.

In discussing Wittgenstein's ruminations on GE Moore's 'common sense' attempted refutation of scepticism about empirical propositions (e.g. 'I know that there is a living human body which is my body'), D.Z. Phillips identifies six characteristics that such basic propositions share:

'(a) these propositions seem free from the possibility of error; (b) they are not hypotheses; (c) they are not based on experience but show themselves in experience; (d) they are rarely formulated but are involved in ways in which we do formulate propositions in the course of our activities; (e) when people in our culture are cut off from these propositions which we take for granted and do not question, we do not say that they are mistaken, but that they must be joking or insane; (f) these propositions do not enjoy their status because of their inherent nature: changes in the culture in which we live can bring about changes in the norms of what we do and do not regard as reasonable.'[17]

Swinburne, offering a similar taxonomy, distinguishes two sorts of propositions:

'Some of the propositions which a man believes, he believes solely on the grounds of other propositions which he believes, and which, he believes, make the former probable; but some of the propositions which a man believes, he does not believe only for this reason. I believe that a train will leave Oxford for Birmingham tomorrow at 1.11 am solely because it says that it will on the timetable and railway timetables are on the whole reliable (which latter propositions I believe). Yet my belief that the clock says that it is 5.10 is not something which I believe for the sole reason that it is made probable by others of my beliefs (e.g. my beliefs that it is now 5.10 and that clocks in this house are usually reliable). On the contrary, I believe that the clock says that it is now 5.10 because it looks to me as if it does say 5.10. My system of beliefs has here an anchorage in what I believe to be my experience of the world.

'I shall call those propositions which seem to a man to be true and which he is inclined to believe, but not solely on the ground that they are made probable by other propositions which he believes, his basic propositions.'[18]

Foundationalism then is the belief that every proposition we are justified in believing is justified, in part, because of some relation that it bears to the directly evident. The propositions which constitute this foundation of belief are not derivable from other propositions, they are self-evident. A simple criterion for a proposition being a basic proposition is that it is possible to know the proposition (p) but not to be able to produce evidence that p. In other words, they are believed (and rightly so) without evidence. Consider Aristotle's axiom: if p then p (the Principle of Identity). How could one possibly hope to substantiate or prove this? Such things as the truth of basic propositions are just seen and, moreover, to believe them is rational.

Anthony Kenny adds to the criteria for foundational basicality (self-evident and evident to the senses) that to be truly basic a belief might also be 'fundamental' or be evident 'to memory' or be 'defensible by argument, inquiry, or performance'. Kenny's nuance of the classical position is doubtless right, but I shall not pursue it here. He contends that the classical position is 'self-refuting': 'in that this criterion for rational belief seems to be itself neither self-evident nor evident to the senses, nor is it easy to see by what process of reasoning it could be derived from such premises'[19]. He argues that his modified position is not self-refuting, and again he is right. (Kenny's critique brings to mind the refutation of the 'verification principle' of the Logical Positivists: a proposition is meaningful only if it is in principle verifiable. But, by its own criterion, the verification principle is itself meaningless).

It is easy to see that I might believe that it is raining when in fact it is not. But how can one believe that (or calculate that, or be misled into thinking that, etc.) the square of 18 is 256? There is no possible world in which the square of 18 is 256, and so the sentence '18 squared = 256' does not have truth conditions, and so does not express a proposition.

The question of self-evidence is much debated in foundational theory. If I believe a necessary proposition p, say, 2+2 = 4, without proof or evidence, then a foundationalist ought to construe it as a necessary proposition which is not a basic proposition because it is neither a proposition which is forced on me by my experience of the world or by reason, nor do I know it; I simply believe that it is a necessary proposition. But just how is this self-evident? What of: 'an angle in a semicircle is a right angle'? Is this a self-evident proposition? We might agree that a self-evident truth must necessarily be true, but self-evidence also seems to suggest a notion of obviousness that 'necessarily true' does not. What is obvious to one person is not obvious to another and what appears to many to be indubitable is not necessarily true. The idea of self-evidence is indeed rather vague and comes down in the end to believing that if one understands a proposition to be self-evident then that is enough for seeing that it is necessarily true. Just what 'seeing' is here is difficult, but it is obvious that some will not see the truth of some necessarily true propositions which truth others do see. Although I do not wish to engage in the debate, I would like to suggest that it is the complexity of the necessarily true proposition which will determine just how easily its truth can be seen.

Many Foundationalists would argue that belief in God is not a basic proposition in that:

a) it might be false, therefore it is not necessary,

and
b) it is only known on the basis of other propositions, i.e., it is not obvious in the way that self-evident propositions are;
c) it is not evident to the senses.

In short, belief in God is *only* belief; it is not self-evident nor is it necessary, nor is it forced on one by one's experience of the world, therefore it is not a basic proposition. Therefore, belief in God cannot be foundational (I shall put aside here the question that it is perfectly rational to hold beliefs which are neither self-evident nor evident to the senses, e.g. Canberra is the capitol of Australia).

Suppose that we accept that the proposition that 2+2 = 4 is self-evident. Is it self-evident because it is true? Well, yes and no. It would not be self-evident if it *appeared* to be false, but its truth is not truth established on the grounds of probability, or because there is good evidence that 2+2 = 4, because 2+2 = 4 is true in every possible world. So, the fact that 2+2 = 4 is true no doubt inclines us to feel that it is self-evident. But is it not more pertinent to say that it's being self-evident is what inclines us to believe it is true? In other words, it is the fact that the truth of 2+2 = 4 stares us in the face which makes it self-evident. Accordingly, it cannot be argued that whatever appears to be self-evident is true is a self-evident truth because this does not give us a reason for distinguishing between apparent and actual self-evidence. The claim that whatever appears to be self-evident is true is a self-evident truth, may or may not be true; but it is no ground for accepting the proposition that whatever appears to be self-evident is true is a self-evident truth unless we already accept that proposition. That something appears to be self-evident is no guarantee of self-evidence.

It seems to me either that one simply accepts a proposition as self-evident or not. Some will accept some propositions as self-evident and others, other propositions; and that some are obviously acceptable to one and not to others may have to do with their complexity or some such thing. Whatever the reason, it is simply a matter that a person who accepts propositions as self-evident is committed to that acceptance because they appear to her to be self-evident. That is, she trusts what appears to her to be the case. But what is it that she trusts here? Surely nothing other than herself. She trusts her own ability to make basic propositions which form the foundation of every other proposition she holds. Nor is it *unreasonable* for her to do so, even though she cannot justify her trust by producing other, more basic, propositions as evidence. So only propositions which are self-evident or necessarily true or which are mediated by our perception of the world are basic propositions, but what is self-evident is something which is simply accepted on trust, or, dare I say, on faith.

Because belief in God is not, for Foundationalists, basic, then religious beliefs will simply be propositions dependent on evidence and accorded some degree of probability. In other words, we are back in the realm of the God hypothesis.

3. Reformed Epistemology

So-called Reformed Epistemologists argue that belief in God is among our foundational, or basic, propositions. Believing in God is of a kind with believing in the existence of the external world and such belief is no more amenable to the production of evidence in its support than is the belief in the existence of the external world.

Alvin Plantinga (1932 -), as we have seen, is an American philosopher of whom the *Oxford Companion to Philosophy* says: '... he used contemporary modal logic and metaphysics to formulate a valid ontological argument for the existence of God [in *The Nature of Necessity*, 1974]'. As well as teaching at Yale and Notre Dame, Plantinga taught at Calvin College. It is presumably in reference to the latter that we get the name 'Reformed'.

In *God and Other Minds* (1967), Plantinga argued that belief in God and belief in other minds are epistemologically equivalent. And in *Warrant and Proper Function* (1993) and *Warranted Christian*

Belief (2000), he argued that belief in God, not based on propositional evidence, is rational. Throughout, Plantinga's arguments depend on, or are, arguments from analogy. Plantinga shows that this is viable.

In expounding Reformed Epistemology, Plantinga says:

'Suppose we say that the assemblage of beliefs a person holds, together with the various logical and epistemic relations that hold among them, constitutes a person's *noetic structure*. Now ... for each person S there is a set F of beliefs such that a proposition p is rational or rationally acceptable for S only if p is evident with respect to F – only if, that is, the propositions in evidence constitute, on balance, evidence for p. Let us say that this set F of propositions is the *foundation of S's noetic structure*. On this view every noetic structure has a foundation; and a proposition is rational for S, or known by S, or certain for S, only if it stands in the appropriate relation to the foundation of S's noetic structure. Suppose we call this view *foundationalism* ... Might it not be that my belief in God is itself in the foundations of my noetic structure? Perhaps it is a member of F, in which case, of course, it will automatically be evident with respect to F.'[20]

And later he tells us:

'The propositions in F, of course, are not inferred

from other propositions and are not accepted on the basis of other propositions. I know the propositions of my noetic structure, but not by virtue of knowing *other* propositions; for these are the ones I start with. And so the question the foundationalist asks about belief in God, namely, what is the evidence for it – is not properly asked about the members of F; these items don't require to be evident with respect to other propositions in order to be rationally believed. Accordingly, says the foundationalist, not just any proposition is capable of functioning foundationally; to be so capable with respect to a person S, a proposition must not need the evidential support of other propositions; it must be such that it is possible that S knew p but have no evidence for p.'[21]

As we have seen, the question of how one can establish that basic propositions are self-evident is much debated. But it seems clear that the self-evidence of self-evident propositions is something that cannot be proven. As Plantinga shows: the proposition that what seems to be self-evident is very likely to be true is something a foundationalist takes on *trust*, or, we might say, on *faith*. After all, there can *eo ipso* be no justifying propositions *beyond* or *beneath* basic propositions.

But the failure of the Foundationlist to supply a *reason* for proper basicality is shared by the theist who wants to include his belief in God as among his basic propositions. According to Plantinga, and strictly speaking, belief in the existence of God is not properly basic: 'It is not the relatively high level and general proposition *God exists* that is properly basic, but instead propositions detailing some of his attributes and actions'[22]. If Plantinga is right, this would accord with New Testament practice where we saw that the early church showed no interest in the existence of God *per se* but always spoke in terms of his attributes and actions. But belief in God may, even if basic, be corrigible: a theist might become an atheist and *vice versa*. After all, the Foundationalist uses reason to give a foundation for distinguishing between what is reasonable and what is not in our thought.

Of the Foundationalist, Plantinga says:

'He means to commit himself to reason and to nothing more; he therefore declares irrational any noetic structure that contains more – belief in God, for example – in its foundations. But here there is no reason for the theist to follow his example; the believer is not obliged to take his word for it. So far we have found no reason at all for excluding belief in God from the foundations; so far we have found no reason at all for believing that belief in God cannot be basic in a rational noetic structure. To accept belief in God as basic is clearly not irrational in the sense of being proscribed by reason or in conflict with the deliverances of reason. The dictum that belief in God is not basic in a rational noetic structure is neither apparently self-evident nor apparently incorrigible. Nor does it seem to be a deductive consequence of what is self-evident or incorrigible. Is there, then, any reason at all for holding that a noetic structure including belief in God as basic is irrational? If there is, it remains to be specified.'[23]

So, for Plantinga, there are no good reasons to show why belief in God cannot be regarded as among our basic propositions. We might ask: are there no good reasons to show why belief in fairies at the bottom of my garden cannot be regarded as a basic proposition? Plantinga's answer is: '... to recognize that *some* kinds of belief are properly basic ... doesn't for a moment commit one to thinking all *other* kinds are'[24]. Belief in fairies originates in some kind of cognitive error and, as such, is not a *warranted* belief and therefore not basic.

Plantinga's quest is to discover the truth of what *can* be known. Wittgenstein, as we shall see, has no interest in this, rather he wants to understand the *ways* in which we know and in seeing where the bedrock lies in our thought. Plantinga wants to identify the truth operating in epistemic practices and in our noetic structure. Wittgenstein has no such interest.

Plantinga wants to argue that the grounds for believing that God is among our basic propositions are every bit as sound as those of propositions about the external world. Soundness does it not enter the picture for Wittgenstein.

In reading Plantinga, one is left with the feeling that he is trying to turn religious belief into epistemological theories; this is particularly striking in *Warranted Christian Belief* where he contends that we have natural cognitive faculties that enable us to form basic beliefs about God, including the proposition that: 'By virtue of the inward instigation of the Holy Spirit, we see that the teachings of Scripture are true'[25]. What is here proposed is an epistemology which is religious in character but there can be only one theory of knowledge, reflecting one reality.

If Reformed Epistemologists have a point, then atheists and theists are not so much disagreeing as singing different parts from the same hymn sheet. But we must consider the possibility that attempting to provide warrant for our basic propositions is itself confused; this is Wittgenstein's way.

4. *Wittgenstein's Way*

For Wittgenstein, the gap between belief and unbelief is a *grammatical* one: it is embedded in the language of a form of life that goes to make up belief or unbelief. The beliefs of the person of faith are not the same certainties as the beliefs of a person in, say, the natural sciences:

'Our craving for generality has another main source: our preoccupation with the method of science. I mean the method of reducing the explanation of natural phenomena to the smallest possible number of primitive natural laws; and, in mathematics, of unifying the treatment of different topics by using a generalization. Philosophers constantly see the method of science before their eyes, and are irresistibly tempted to ask and answer questions in the way science does. This tendency is the real source of metaphysics, and leads the philosopher into complete darkness. I want to say here that it can never be our job to reduce anything to anything, or to explain anything. Philosophy really *is* "purely descriptive".'[26]

For the later Wittgenstein, that facts come to be regarded as entities or things is unfortunate. When we begin to see the world as a cluster of facts, we entertain a confusion between facts and propositions. But because language utilises or consists in part of propositions, and these somehow 'correspond' to facts, then that which can be given in units (propositions) 'mirrors' that which must itself be made up of units, i.e. the world can be divided into facts. 'Reality' or 'what is the case' or 'some state of affairs' is not what gives language sense. What is the case shows itself in the sense that propositions have. We have a feeling that a fact is somehow objective - out there - self-subsistent and intact, no matter what we say or do, and yet, in so thinking, what we overlook is that very way in which we *see* a fact. I might not see certain 'facts' the way I do, or even see them at all, if I did not already have certain forms of comprehension available to me; and these I take from language, e.g. consider, in Orwell's *1984*, Big Brother's departments' attempt to eliminate thought-crime by the introduction of Newspeak.

If we say of a proposition (p) that it 'agrees with reality' or 'corresponds with the facts' *of what* are we saying this? In a discussion of the application of the calculus of truth-functions to propositions, Wittgenstein says:

'At bottom, giving "This is how things are" as the general form of propositions is the same as giving the definition: a proposition is whatever can be true or false. For instead of "This is how things are" I could have said "This is true". (Or again "This is false".) But we have

"p" is true = p
"p" is false = not p.

'And to say that a proposition can be true or false amounts to saying: we call something a proposition when *in our language* we apply the calculus of truth functions to it.

'Now it looks as if the definition – a proposition is whatever can be true or false- determined what a proposition was, by saying: what fits the concept 'true', or what the concept 'true' fits, is a proposition. So it is as if we had a concept of true and false, which we could use to determine what is and what is not a proposition. What *engages* with the concept of truth (as with a cogwheel), is a proposition.

'But this is a bad picture. It is as if one were to say "The king in chess is *the* piece that one can check." But this can mean no more than that in our game of chess we only check the king. Just as the proposition that only a *proposition* can be true or false can say no more than that we only predicate "true" and "false" of what we call a proposition. And what a proposition is is in one sense determined by the rules of sentence formation (in English for example), and in another sense by the use of the sign in the language-game. And the use of the words "true" and "false" may be among the constituent parts of this game; and if so it *belongs* to our concept "proposition" but does not "fit" it. As we might also say, check *belongs* to our concept of the king in chess (as so to speak a constituent part of it). To say that check did not *fit* our concept of the pawns, would mean that a game in which pawns were checked, in which, say, the players who lost their pawns lost, would be uninteresting or stupid or too complicated or something of the kind.'[27]

Let us take 'the cat is on the mat' as the 'p' of Wittgenstein's passage here. We then get:

p = 'the cat is on the mat'
'p' is true = 'the cat is on the mat' corresponds with
the-cat's-being-on-the-mat.

This latter equation brings out the comparison of the proposition with the actual occurrence, which is supposed to be involved in 'the fact that' statements and in the use of truth predication (i.e. in the correspondence theory of truth at least). Here, the-cat's-being-on-the-mat is taken as 'fitting' or 'corresponding' with p. We would need to say, if we adopted a correspondence theory of truth, that the correspondence of the-cat's-being-on-the-mat with p somehow says that it is true that the cat is on the mat. But it is precisely this view that Wittgenstein wants to criticise: the correspondence of the-cat's-being-on-the-mat with p is seen as somehow 'fitting', or the former is seen as giving the truth of p; but this tells us no more than that we only predicate 'true' and 'false' in such an instance. We have no independent grasp of what 'truth' and 'falsity' are such that these stand as objective criteria enabling us to determine what is or is not a proposition. The proposition 'p is true' can only be understood if one understands what place in the structure of propositional language the sign 'p' has. Moreover, to say in 'p is true', p corresponds with the-cat's-being-on-the-mat, is only to claim that I am correctly asserting p: I am playing the game correctly. This is what Wittgenstein means when he says 'the use of the words "true" and "false" may also be among the constituent parts of the game; and if so it *belongs* to our concept "proposition" but does not "fit" it.' This draws our attention to the conditions under which we are entitled to assert p. Under what conditions are we entitled to assert p (anything) which is rooted in something independent of p? Here we must guard against the danger of supposing there to be some extra-linguistic, independent criteria that give us insight into the relation between assertions and those 'things' that assertion is about. The things we want to make assertions about *could* 'articulate themselves differently'[28]. It is in this sense that 'facts' are, as P.T. Geach has put it, something of an ontological nightmare. Waismann suggests:

'There is a group of words such as "fact", "event", "situation", "case", "circumstance", which display a queer sort of behaviour. One might say of such words that they serve as pegs: it's marvellous what a lot of things you can put on them ("the fact that…"). So they are very handy; but as one focuses on them and asks, e.g., "What is a fact?", they betray a tendency of melting away. The peg-aspect is by far the most important of all. It's just as in the case of the word "reality": in reality, e.g., "in reality" is an adverb.'[29]

A part of what I take Waismann to be saying is that we cannot distinguish between our experience of the world and the way we speak about the world.

Doubts about the existence of the external world are not settled by strength of numbers but by reference to reasons which show how or why one might be mistaken on a given occasion. And the reasons that are relevant are the ones that relate to the conventional standards of making assertions in language about the existence of objects. My ability to have such experiences, say, of seeing a cat on a mat, is not only a matter of my having certain visual sensations. Phillips makes the point in speaking of Geach's comments on sensory perception:

'Geach points out that one important source of the temptation to say that it is my mind that thinks, sees, hears, feels, etc., is the fact that words like "pain" and "seeing" can stand for private experiences. From the undeniable reality of such experiences, some philosophers draw the fallacious conclusion that giving meaning to these words is itself a private experience. As Geach says, this conclusion "is really nonsense: if a sentence I hear or utter contains the word 'pain', do I help myself to grasp its sense by giving myself a pain? As Wittgenstein said, to think that you get the concept of pain by having a pain is like thinking you get the concept of minus quantity by running up an overdraft." The point of Geach's argument here is not to deny that there are private experiences or to advance a behaviouristic thesis, although many will take him to be doing that, in the same way they mistakenly thought Wittgenstein to be doing this before him. But, as Geach says, "It is not a question of whether seeing is (sometimes) a private experience, but whether one can attach meaning to the verb 'to see' by a private uncheckable performance; and this is what I maintain one cannot do to any word at all".[30]

Rai Gaita, in an exposition of Wittgenstein on epistemic propositions, expresses this point differently:

'The further we move (in the hope of seeing the world 'as from no place within it') from what we judge to be merely accidental and local, the more attenuated becomes our sense of the concepts with which we describe what is within our epistemic reach and also *of what it is for something to be within our (or an ideally rational being's) epistemic reach.* It means that our understanding of what it could be for other creatures to think, feel, speak, etc., is inexpungeably anthropocentric. Not, however, in the bad sense of that term which suggests a failure to see things as they are.'[31]

John Gray accuses Wittgenstein of Idealism:

'... Heidegger and Wittgenstein... claimed that the world is a construction of human thought... Wittgenstein believed that his later thought had transcended traditional philosophy, but at bottom it is not much more than another version of the oldest of philosophies – Idealism. For idealists, thought is the final reality; there is nothing that is independent of mind. In practice, this means that the world is a human invention.'[32]

Idealism is the metaphysical doctrine that reality is fundamentally mental in nature. But Wittgenstein never maintained that what is real is confined to our minds or their contents. In spite of Gray's equivocating 'at bottom', 'not much more than' and 'in practice', Wittgenstein held no such view; he had no doubt that he found himself in a world that was not of his making. Indeed, it is the generalized abstraction of Idealism that Wittgenstein wishes to oppose. In his examination of actual cases of beliefs, sensations, etc., in our social lives, Wittgenstein is actually trying to undermine the Cartesian picture of a solipsistic world of *any* person's creating.

'Knowing God' or 'seeing God', or even 'seeing that there is a God' cannot be a matter only of having experienced God, of having had certain sensory experiences. To assume that is to assume that existential assertions are inferences from statements of experience. The difference between seeing God and seeing a cat on a mat has to do with the fact that the public conventions governing how they are understood are different and depend on the fact that there are such concepts as 'a God who acts' or 'a living God' available.

It is sometimes objected that although the

public conventions generally applied to existential statements concerning cats and mats are almost universally accepted, this is not the case with existential statements about God. A large number of people do not agree on the criteria or simply do not share them; they are not public in the way that the conventions relating to physical objects are. As Basil Mitchell remarks:

'As [Hick] remarks, "It is a basic truth in or presupposition of our language that it is rational or sane to believe in the reality of the external world that we inhabit in common with other people, and irrational and insane not to do so". It is not simply that we find ourselves under a psychological compulsion to believe in a world of things and persons; there is no coherent alternative. It is for this reason that the sceptical argument from illusion fails. In order to recognise an illusion for what it is we have to assume that our perceptual judgements are generally reliable; and this is an assumption which, because of the centrality of things and persons in any conceivable worldview, we necessarily make. So long as the existence of God is presupposed, it will be true that, in precisely a similar way, we shall not be able to use the possibility that some encounters with God are illusory as a reason for denying that a particular one is genuine. But the presupposition in this case is one that can be challenged and, therefore, requires a defence.'[33]

But just how is one going to go about challenging this presupposition? Are we not here back with the question of what it means 'to see that there is a God'?

To understand the operation of belief statements construed as propositions we need to understand something about the difference between the sense of an expression and its reference. If one has grasped the sense of a sentence one has thereby understood the conditions under which would be true. So, for example, when we understand the simple word 'paper', we do not simply know what the sound refers to, its referent, we understand the conditions under which things are called 'paper'. For example, I call something paper if I think it is a writing material made of a certain substance. The application of a name to a referent involves my holding certain beliefs about it. If it is the case that the beliefs I hold about paper are not shared by others, then my use of 'paper' will not be understood by others. This shows that any account of sense must be given not at the level of individual speakers (i.e. an account of the sense of an expression within a particular idiolect) but at the level of a linguistic community (i.e. an account of the sense of an expression within a language). Quite simply: sense is not to do with knowledge on an individual level but rather with knowledge possessed by a community of speakers of the language.

Now when it comes to religion, we find that it is ridden with statements, apparently propositions, where the set of beliefs which we share about everyday objects and which makes it possible to understand cultures other than our own, is abandoned, or greatly modified. The failure to recognise this lies at the heart of some cognitivist approaches to faith so that belief is construed as propositions which can be moulded into arguments of a deductive or inductive nature which will work (or not as the case may be) only on the assumption that they have the same sort of sense of other, non-religious deductive or inductive arguments: the Mackie and Swinburne approach.

What sense then can we see conveyed in a statement of religious belief? The answer is to be found if we examine attitudes to the content of propositions rather than simply looking at the apparent sense of propositions. We have seen that in 'believe' we have an expression of an attitude to truth. This attitude we may call 'tone'. It is possible to understand the sense of religious beliefs in terms not only of their truth conditions, but also of their tone, their evocational, instinctive, expressive use in a particular community, as part of the cultus.

There can be no doubt of the evocational power of religious utterances. Consider, for example, the words of the Mass: 'This is my body'. Many regard this as a piece of magico-ritualistic mumbo-jumbo. An historical or linguistic analysis of such statements surely will not give a complete or adequate picture of what such sayings mean for the believer who utters or hears them. An historical analysis may show the origins and associations of such statements but it will not explain why those who engage in such rites and say such things continue to do so. A linguistic analysis, in a wider context than the utterance itself, makes plain in part its symbolic nature but will not account for what I have called attitudes to truth or tone, which is part of the meaning of the expression. To understand such utterances, it would be necessary to show how it evokes emotions, expresses attitudes to truth, aspirations, fears, hopes as well as historical beliefs and general semantic features of such utterances. Nor do I mean that the utterance is only the expression of an instinct or emotion, or even mainly this. The subtlety, complexity, formality of so many rites and accompanying beliefs cannot be accounted for in these terms alone, as Phillips shows:

'"This is my body" is not a reason given to explain God's saving grace but an expression of it. God's saving grace, shown in the Eucharist, is not knowledge in the way that deductions may be drawn from bedrock propositions is; it is not derived from evidence; it is not an opinion held by the priest who utters these words; they do not require reasons to justify them; they are not made more true by a degree of probability.... Whereas "belief" in connection with empirical propositions may express a degree of uncertainty, such that it makes sense to respond by saying, "Oh, you only believe", to respond in such a way to a man who said, "I believe in God" would be to misunderstand the use of "believe" in this religious context.'[34]

There are, of course, differences between certain bedrock propositions and religious propositions: a failure to accept the veracity of certain bedrock propositions (e.g. 'This is a hand') is what we call madness. But someone who wishes to deny religious propositions cannot be said to be mad. But here we have to be careful about what is being denied when one is said to deny a religious proposition. Wittgenstein says:

'Suppose that someone believed in the Last Judgement, and I don't, does this mean that I believe the opposite to him, just that there won't be such a thing? I would say: "not at all, or not always" … Would you say: "I believe the opposite", or "There is no reason to suppose such a thing?" I'd say neither... There are instances where you have faith – where you say "I believe" – and on the other hand this belief does not rest on the fact on which our ordinary everyday beliefs normally do rest... If you ask me whether or not I believe in a Judgement

Day, in the sense in which religious people have belief in it, I wouldn't say: "No. I don't believe there will be such a thing." It would seem to me utterly crazy to say this.'[35]

The belief in the Last Judgement cannot be falsified or denied as if it were a defeasible hypothesis because it is no such thing. A denial of such a belief is better understood as an indication that such beliefs mean nothing to one or that one does not have such beliefs informing one's life.

That 'God exists' is a bedrock proposition is suggested by the fact that it is just as odd that it should be said as saying 'Trees exist'. 'God exists' is not part of the language of faith any more than 'Trees exist' is part of the normal language of arborists. Even Anselm, in concluding his ontological argument says: 'And this being thou art, our Lord, our God'. This is not a conclusion to the ontological argument but a postscript arising from an already held belief that only will ill-will could deny. To ponder 'God exists' is to wonder whether there is any point in praying and praising and it is in the observation of these that illumination lies.

Faith is not belief without adequate evidence, nor is it a blind trust in unproven propositions. To assume that either is the case is to assume that there are some criteria of adequate evidence, or that there is some proof of propositions, that can be applied to religious belief and which will allow of definite or probable conclusions. If, however, my argument concerning the shift of meaning via tonal attitudes to truth is viable, then such external criteria are wanting. Indeed, they are inappropriate.

While Wittgenstein did not deny the bedrock nature of basic propositions, he was more interested in how we can make sense of them. Wittgenstein does not contend that bedrock propositions are the foundations on which other propositions lie: they are simply taken for granted, part of the warp and weft of our discourse and behaviour. They are rarely questioned except in a rarefied philosophical context; otherwise, we learn basic propositions in the context of learning in general. A child is not taught of an *existing* cow, she is simply (ostensively) shown the picture of the cow, with the accompanying word 'cow'.

The building blocks of propositions – which itself is not taught – is what Wittgenstein calls a world-picture. This world-picture is not basic, in the foundational sense, but manifests itself in *what* we say and *the way we say it*.

Basic propositions do not, for Wittgenstein, give rise to doubts or speculation: he is not interested in the *knowable*; he is content simply to investigate bedrock propositions as part of the deep grammar of our common language.

Wittgenstein is often mistaken for a Reformed Epistemologist and I am not here concerned with exegesis of his works. It is enough to say that I believe this constitutes a misreading of his epistemology and particularly of his most sustained consideration of any topic, *On Certainty*. Nuances between Reformed Epistemology and Wittgenstein aside: they open up possibilities in understanding religious belief, not as failed hypotheses, a set of extrapolations from the world to God, but as faith in foundations which seek no further justification. Belief in God entails belief in the object of faith, but that does not mean that God is an object in the way that his creation consists of objects. That is why 'faith seeking understanding' is characteristic of some forms of religious belief but 'understanding seeking faith' is characteristic of none. Beliefs entailing trust in a God who acts should not be seen as a set of explanations traceable to initial premises postulating God as an hypothesis. Something can constitute an explanation without being an hypothesis.

For Wittgenstein, the task of the philosopher is descriptive and her aim is clarification. In his famous dictum: *philosophy leaves everything as it is.*

Mary Geach tells of her mother's, Elizabeth Anscombe's, comments about the dying Wittgenstein: he said to her that he loved truth[36]. But this is often misinterpreted to mean he tried to set forth principles or attempted to develop an epistemology (of everything). He didn't. Geach reports her mother saying of Wittgenstein: 'He had said to her that this was the difference he had made to philosophy: philosophy books before him were either about epistemology, or had titles about the principles of something or other. The question then is: how can one be doing philosophy if one neither tries to set forth the most general principles nor to found everything on one's own infallible perceptions?'[37]

Phillips offers this description of Wittgenstein's method:

'These fundamental problems... are *logical* in character. They have had to do with Wittgenstein's treatment of basic propositions, a treatment which does justice to their fundamental character without falling into the pitfalls of foundationalism. For Wittgenstein, the basic propositions he discusses are not the foundations or presuppositions of the ways we think, and neither can the ways in which we think be derived or inferred from them. Rather, the basic propositions are held fast by all that surrounds them. They are not the bases *on* which our ways of thinking depend (foundationalism), but are basic *in* our ways of thinking.'[38]

The type of thinking involved in which we reach what Wittgenstein calls bedrock is not itself grounded in anything more fundamental. Bedrock propositions are groundless. Here we can only say: that language game is played. But Wittgenstein goes on to say: 'a language game is only possible if one trusts something.'[39]

The notions of right and wrong do not apply in respect of belief and unbelief. We can only say, with Wittgenstein, that this language-game is played. Whether God exists or not is, essentially, a trivial question. Indeed, most metaphysical speculation (when thinking of ontology in ethics, for example) is trivial. Belief is a minor part of the complex matrix of all those things which go together to make up the commitment we call faith.

Notes:

1. pp. 29-46, *Canadian Journal of Philosophy*, Vol. II, No. 1.
2. See Appendix 1, *Aristotle's Theology.*
3. p. 115, *Language, Truth and Logic*, Gollancz, 1949.
4. pp. 85-86, *Faith and Reason*, Columbia University Press, 1983.
5. p. 738, *A New History of Western Philosophy*, OUP, 2010.
6. p. 12, *Religion Without Explanation*, Blackwell, 1976.
7. *op. cit.* p. 18.
8. *op. cit.* p. 22.
9. p. 1, *The Miracle of Theism*, Clarendon, 1982.

10. *loc. cit.*

11. p. 92, 'Evil and Omnipotence', in *The Philosophy of Religion,* (ed.) B. Mitchell, OUP, 1971.

12. p. 29, Remarks on Frazer's "Golden Bough", in *The Human World*, No. 3, May, 1971.

13. *op. cit.* p. 36.

14. Allen Lane, 2018.

15. *op. cit.* p. 11.

16. *loc. cit.*

17. *op. cit.* p. 162f.

18. pp. 19-20, *Faith and Reason,* Clarendon, 1981.

19. p. 25, *Faith and Reason*, Columbia University Press, 1983.

20. pp. 12-13, 'Is Belief in God Rational?' in CF Delaney (ed.) *Rationality and Religious Belief,* University of Notre Dame Press, 1979.

21. *loc. cit.*

22. *op. cit.* p. 81.

23. p. 344, *Warranted Christian Belief*, OUP, 2000. Plantinga's answer to this question is convoluted, to say the least, but merits consideration.

24. *op.* cit. p. 26.

25. *op.* cit. OUP, 2000, p. 180.

26. p. 18, *The Blue and Brown Books*, Blackwell, 1969.

27. *Philosophical Investigations*, 136.

28. cf. F. Waismann, 'Verifiability' in *Logic and Language*, (ed.) A. Flew, Blackwell, 1968.

29. *op. cit.* pp. 136-137.

30. p. 4, *Death and Immortality*, Macmillan, 1970. Quotations from Geach are from *God and the Soul*, R & KP, 1969, pp. 19 – 20.

31. p. 168, *Good and Evil, an Absolute Conception*, Routledge, 2nd edition, 2004.

32. p. 53, *Straw Dogs*, Granta, 2002.

33. pp. 108ff, *The Justification of Religious Belief*, Macmillan, 1973.

34. p. 164, *Religion Without Explanation.*

35. p. 53ff, *Lectures and Conversations on Aesthetics, Psychology and Religious Belief*, Blackwell, 1970.

36. p. xvi, *From Plato to Wittgenstein*, Imprint Academic, 2011.

37. p. xviii, *op. cit.*

38. p. 123, *Faith after Foundationalism.*

39. *On Certainty*, 509.

17

Religious Ethics and the Ethics of Unbelief

There can be no such thing as religious, let alone Christian, ethics. Ethics is beyond sectarianism. More particularly, Jesus' teaching: *The Kingdom of Heaven is at hand. Repent and prepare*, is hardly a basis for ethical ruminations. A mistaken apocalyptic warning with its double imperative is no foundation at all for considerations about how one should live. And for me, as it was for Socrates, how one should live must constitute the starting, if not the end, point for moral philosophy.

Unbelief has no more insight to offer about ethics than does belief.

I shall use 'ethics' (Greek: *ethikos* = arising from habit) and 'morality' (Latin: *moralis* = from *mos* = the will or inclination of a person) interchangeably.

What Ethics is Not

If the literature which bears on reality were given a place in the landscape of our thought, 'moral theory' would constitute an enclave, if not a ghetto.

In Plato's *Euthyphro*, Socrates poses his interlocutor a question: 'Is that which is holy loved by the gods because it is holy or is it holy because it is loved by the gods?' (10 a). For Socrates, the answer lies in the protasis: the gods love it because it is holy.

John Gray contends that any sort of absolutism in ethics depends on belief in God: it is holy because it is loved by the gods.

Socrates or Gray?

Gray is critical of Platonism and universals in morality:

'Without a law-giver, what can a universal moral law mean? If you think of morality as part of the natural behaviour of the human animal, you find that humans do not live according to a single moral code. Unless you think one of them has been mandated by God, you must accept the variety of moralities as part of what it means to be human.'[1]

Absolutist ethicists believe that moral qualities inhere intrinsically in our actions. It would be not inaccurate to say that, prior to Bentham, absolutism, since Plato, has been the prevailing conception in moral philosophy. But absolute demands are alien to English sentiment. Much of this arises from the mature English inclination to amateurism, to tolerance and to a deep-seated suspicion of the trenchant totalitarian ideologies that arose on the Continent after 1789 (consider why England has only ever once been touched by Civil War and that the one that it had, at least by

Continental standards, was particularly benign).

Many religious people have no problem with the idea of absolute demands – and these are usually prohibitions - because these, they believe and as Gray says, are part of the corpus of God's revelation: *thou shalt not...* Antagonists argue that this absolutism obstructs or nullifies necessary discussion about the consequences of such commitments. But nothing whatever of all this has to be true of absolute judgements in ethics.

I have in mind here identifying religion as, say, Paul Tillich's 'ultimate concern'; this kind of criteriological assessment helps to point up the absolute nature of *both* the ideal *and* the demands of religion, and the same can be seen in ethics.

The liberal consequentialist, with an eye on the past, is suspicious of absolute injunctions knowing only too well what they have led, and might lead, to. But these need not be the only, or indeed the principal, considerations. *Consequentialism* is the school of moral philosophy which takes all actions to be right or wrong in virtue of the value of their consequences; *utilitarianism* is the best-known form of consequentialism. Consequentialists are inclined to adduce what are called 'hard cases' in order to beat their opponents into submission. One is reminded of the tactics of the Sophists here; this is no new procedure: we find Polus attempting the same thing with Socrates in Plato's *Gorgias*. Socrates has argued that it is better to suffer evil than to do it, to which Polus replies:

'What you mean? If a man is arrested for plotting a dictatorship and racked and castrated and blinded with hot irons and finally, after suffering many other varieties of exquisite torture and seeing his wife and children suffer the same, is crucified or burnt at the stake, will he be happier than if he gets off, establishes himself as dictator and spends the rest of his life in power doing as he chooses, the object and envy and admiration to natives and foreigners alike? Is that what you maintain that it is impossible to prove untrue?' (473c)

This kind of procrastination goes against the grain: the reason it does is not that these 'hard cases' are trivial and offensive, although that certainly is the case, but that the demand for ruminations on consequences misleads us into the trap of a shallow apprehension of the lives and responses of those involved; they actually remove the evil (both evil inflicted and evil suffered), as opposed to the harm, from the story.

L. A.'s Trolley Cars

It takes very little intellectual ingenuity to fashion a tolerably clean 'hard case', like that of Polus, to confute consequentialism itself. The reason it should refute consequentialism is that consequences are not morally relevant considerations in certain circumstances.

The trolley case, first proposed by Philippa Foot, runs thus: there is a trolley whose brakes have failed with (say) now five people on the track ahead. The bank is too steep for them to escape. This doesn't go to the issue of humanly-induced evil, but we can see that as a benefit. In the end, it can be cited to say something about consequentialism which is crucial. The purpose of these cases is to explore moral conceptions and what is at issue is moral relevance. The good news in this bad circumstance is that a bystander at the switch can divert the trolley to the side-track. The bad news is that there is one innocent person on the side-track, equally doomed by the steep grade. Is it morally permissible to switch tracks? To say *no* is to acknowledge and endorse a stringent 'constraint'. To say *yes* is to reply as a consequentialist, because the consequentialist not only may, but must, divert the trolley or run foul of the theory. Perhaps this case shows nothing. Or perhaps, as Elizabeth Anscombe suggested, it shows the moral turpitude of those willing to postulate such cases. But I suggest otherwise. Does a decision not to turn the trolley in respect of a 'constraint' on killing innocents seem to anyone to be the act of a fanatical absolutist in the moral sphere? That is the important question, not: 'what would you do?'

Then I offer a kindred case, one in which five patients need different transferable vital organs which must come from a donor with a very rare blood profile. The good news is that a surgeon has located this individual. The trouble is that the woman in question is young and healthy and will bear children and outlive all the patients in the natural course of events. Is it permissible for the surgeon to kill the one in order to save the lives of the ill five others? I have yet to find someone who thinks it is, short of some criminal incentive. It is simply too absurd.

From the consequentialist point of view the avoidable death of five is, must be, the worst of the two outcomes. But I think we can now catch the consequentialist out in saying *yes* to the trolley case, as the theory requires, and *no* to the transplant case, because the interests of the five patients, however strong, are not morally relevant. Yet what is the pertinent moral difference between the two cases which could account for different answers?

Conrad Johnson, a defender of consequentialism[2] found a 'difference' in that the surgeon is illicitly 'playing God' (itself a very dubious notion), exceeding his moral authority. This is a fatal reply, for it not only concedes an absolute constraint but suggests an absolute source of normativity. But Johnson seems mistaken as to the difference in any event, because whatever one says of the surgeon is true of the bystander in the trolley case. Without another, better answer, we have a rejection of consequentialism, and it is a hardcase which provides the haymaker. It hardly matters if this case is fanciful, but I hasten to add, that except for a few simplifying assumptions, this hard case is not hypothetical; there is a brisk and murderous black market in organs, and the evil that men do may well be done to prevent bad outcomes which have numbers in their favour.

One may think that the transplant case distorts agency. But I think that this serve and volley treatment of the trolley case is clean enough for our purposes, and that it is the consequentialist theory which distorts agency, not the formulation of the case.

For John Gray, 'the roots of ethics are in animal virtues':

'… The importance of morality in our lives is a fiction. We use it in the stories we tell ourselves and others about our lives to give them a sense that they might otherwise lack. But in so doing we obscure the truth of how we live.

'Moral philosophy has always been an exercise in make-believe, less realistic in its picture of human life than the average bourgeois novel. We must look elsewhere if we want anything that approaches the truth.'[3]

And again:

'Western thought is fixated on the gap between what *is* and what *ought to be*. In everyday life we do not scan our options beforehand, then enact the one that is best. We simply deal with whatever is at hand. We get up in the morning and put on our clothes without meaning to do so. We help a friend in just the same way. Different people follow different customs; but in acting without intention, we are not simply following habit. Intentional acts occur in all sorts of situations, including those we have never come across before.'[4]

How different all this is from Iris Murdoch on our moral actions:

'Ignorance, muddle, fear, wishful thinking, lack of tests often make us feel that moral choice is something arbitrary, a matter of the personal will rather than for attentive study. Our attachments tend to be selfish and strong, and the transformation of our lives from selfishness to unselfishness is sometimes hard even to conceive of. Yet is the situation really so different? Should a retarded child be kept at home or sent to an institution? Should an elderly relation who is a troublemaker be cared for or asked to go away? Should an unhappy marriage be continued for the sake of the children? Should I leave my family in order to do political work? Should I neglect them in order to practise my art? Love which brings the right answer is an exercise of justice and realism and really looking... It is a *task* to come to see the world as it is.'[5]

For Gray, there is no *task* involved: life is a series of accommodations governed by custom rather than something that is universal and categorical; but the fact that our lives are framed by this is what makes us human.

We must find some way of considering – or, indeed, of empowering – the place of moral considerations in our lives. Unless we do this, our assessment of human behaviour will be a caricature which would consist, in a fashion not unlike Gray's, of a view of our behaviour as an administrative outlook on life. If someone believes, as Gray appears to do, that our moral behaviour is essentially our ability sensibly to control those areas of our lives where we can affect change – getting up in the morning and putting our clothes on – then our ethical outlook will be essentially administrative. How best to organise the socks drawer. But this misses the point.

The character of our intentions circumscribe ways of achieving them. For on an administrative view of ethics we will see that some means are more effective than others in achieving the desired end: other means will be circumscribed as being irrelevant or unproductive. Thus, if what I want to do is deal appropriately with, say, antisocial behaviour then various suggestions might be made to me about how I could achieve that end. I might be told to call the police; I might be encouraged to close the windows and bolt the doors; I might be told to move house to the South Pole. There will be different views about how to achieve my desired goal but only some means will be seen as relevant as to how best to achieve them. If someone told me to wear a certain coloured tie or take a rest, I might take this as a way of telling me to set aside my goal. Moreover, extrinsic forces, for example the law, will impose their own limits on my behaviour. These kinds of accommodations are in what Gray sees morality to be. But morality lies beyond this.

In spite of Gray's attempt to trivialise morality ('the importance of morality in our lives is a fiction'), there is such a thing as moral worth. We are not only concerned with what we want, but also with the character of our wants and the way we attempt to achieve them. Thus a superordinate constraint of a different order from mean talk of means and purposes will apply to ethical considerations. The limits set by moral considerations constitute what J.L. Stocks calls 'an additional principle of discrimination', because we must account for more than simply ends and means. When our intentions are determined and the means of achieving them decided, we still must know whether what we intend can be done, as Socrates would have it, virtuously, or that what we intend is right, or what intrudes least or causes less offence, or satisfies God, or...

If moral considerations condemn hatred, they also extol love; if they condemn drug-taking, they also commend a healthy lifestyle. Love, health, thoughtfulness and courage – parts of a hierarchy of virtues – are not constraints on moral action but, as Socrates taught, positive virtues and ideals in human life which for many make that life worth living; they are not the mere administrative accommodations Gray contends they are.

It is important to see that where ethics is concerned, the discovery of what must be done often involves one in evil, pain and suffering. A person who cannot see this is one whose life has never touched any depth of relationship or which is fundamentally evil.

More particularly, our values will generally form a coherent whole where one point of certainty supports another. These mutual coherences of the values we feel sure of, and the things we desire, develop the thickening destiny of our lives.

Here we might compare Thucydides on the ultimatum of the Athenians to the men of Melos. The Athenians brushed aside justice and preferred to consider only what means were available to them at the time. But if one's conception of morality, in this case justice, varies with the circumstances then it is likely that whenever one has the power to command, one will do so.

Moral considerations have a superordinate bearing on purposes and their execution. Good and evil are *sui generis.* If that is so, reality stands resplendent and beyond Gray's talk of means and purposes, or worse, custom and intentionless acts.

The Sophists

The poverty of consequentialism was exposed over 2000 years ago in Socrates' refutation of the Sophists (Greek = sages/wise ones). Plato's dialogues are nearly all set in the late fifth century BC. In an increasingly cosmopolitan Athens, new questions were being asked which challenged traditional *mores.*

Great intellectual attention was devoted to the question of the roles in human life of *nomos* and *phusis* – loosely translated 'convention' and 'nature'. Many traditional values and patterns of behaviour, hitherto treated as 'natural', part of the inevitable order of things, were now suddenly thought of as conventional, part of fallible human endeavour which might well have been ordered otherwise; this had a big impact on views about government and other social institutions. And although this debate continues to this day, very little intellectual attention is devoted to it. In fact, the reverse seems to be the case: intellectual conversation is closed down, sometimes violently, and often in the very places where such debate should be encouraged and should flourish: in universities.

These tendencies could lead to cynicism and scepticism about there being right and wrong answers in matters of value; and they were confirmed by a group of intellectually prominent people usually called Sophists; these were not a school of thought but a collection of professional teachers who, for a fee, lectured and gave instruction in various cities, claiming to know how to help people win arguments and generally get on in life. Nowadays, self-help books and 'motivational' speakers fill that particularly shallow niche (sadly, as do academics who teach so-called 'practical ethics').

What the Sophists taught varied, but they nearly all taught the skills of speechmaking and debating (what we now think of as *rhetoric,* Greek: *reetor* = orator), necessary for someone aiming at a public career; they offered the nearest thing to a further education not available in the ancient world until Plato founded his own school, the *Academy*.

Plato presents some of the Sophists in his dialogues, usually in a hostile or ludicrous light; they angered him because they had pretensions to knowledge about how to live one's life, which on examination tended to be useless or vacuous;

but much more because they regarded matters of moral importance as being a matter of amoral expertise, teachable by them for a fee.

Sophists tend to dismiss worries about right and wrong as being without substance, merely a product of one's upbringing. The most famous of them, Protagoras, held just such a kind of relativism about values and much else.

Protagoras

Protagoras (c. 490 – 420 BC) came from Abdera on the north coast of the Aegean, also the birthplace of Democritus. He travelled widely throughout the Greek world, including several visits to Athens, where he was associated with Pericles, who invited him to write the constitution for the Athenian colony of Thurii. The ancient tradition of his condemnation for impiety and flight from Athens is refuted by Plato's evidence (*Meno* 91e) that he enjoyed a universally high reputation till his death and afterwards. He was famous in antiquity for agnosticism concerning the existence and nature of the gods, and for the doctrine that: 'Man is the measure of all things', i.e. the thesis that all sensory appearances and all beliefs are true for the person whose appearance or belief they are. On the most plausible construal, that doctrine attempts to eliminate objectivity and truth altogether. Even in ancient Greece, they lived in a 'post-truth' world. It was attacked by Democritus and Plato (in the *Theaetetus*) on the ground that it is self-refuting: if all beliefs are true, then the belief that it is not the case that all beliefs are true is itself true. While that charge of self-refutation fails because it ignores the relative isolation of truth in the theory, it may be restated as follows: either the theory undermines itself by asserting as an objective truth that there is no objective truth or it merely asserts as a subjective truth that there is no objective truth. But to assert a subjective truth is to make no assertion. So either the theory refutes itself, or it asserts nothing. In the *Protagoras*, Plato represents him as maintaining a fairly conservative form of social morality based on a version of social contract theory: humans need to develop social institutions to survive in a hostile world, and the basic social virtues – justice and self-control – must be generally observed if those institutions are to flourish.

Man is the Measure of All Things

The main purpose of the *Republic* is to show the difference between the just and the unjust life, that is, between a good and evil life (484a). Good and evil stand opposed for Plato in a definite way: the distinction between the two is not an incidental matter which will make little difference to a person's life. It is the one distinction above all others, which it is necessary to make and act upon in order to make life worth living at all. It is because this distinction is so definite that Plato speaks of the destiny of the soul as he does (cf. *Phaedo*, 108aff, *Republic* 617dff).

Protagoras' view, like Gray's, tends to a relativism (allowing for different moralities) which regards the good as expedient, for it does not in any way show, as Plato wishes to do, that there are only two alternatives when we think about human life. For Protagoras there may be innumerable alternatives. His measure of what is good is a human one which allows for different points of view in that whatsoever a person thinks to be good is good to her; the shallow *beauty is in the eye of the beholder* thesis. Plato, however, regards Goodness as not dependent on any human standards which may be different, but something which is divine in nature and unalterable. Goodness is demanded of people, not because it is expedient to seem good, even if one is not, but because 'there is no unrighteousness with God who is perfectly righteous, and there is nothing more like God than one of us who becomes as righteous as possible' (176c).

People who live a life that is characterised by a false show of virtue and consider that other people believe them to be virtuous do not know the penalty for injustice: a life of godless misery; that is the pattern according to which they direct their lives (176e).

Socrates

Socrates died in year 399 BC and since Plato tells us in the *Apology* that he was then 70 years old, he must have been born about 469. He was a citizen of Athens, of the Antiochid tribe and of the *deme* Alopeke. His father, Sophroniscus, was a stonemason, and his mother, Phaenarete, was a midwife. It is likely that he was married twice. Xanthippe was the wife of his later years, and when he died he left two small children and youth called Lamprocles.

From his childhood on, it appears that Socrates was something of an oddity. He had a startling physical appearance: snub-nosed, bearded, bald, with bulbous and glaring eyes, which he had a peculiar habit of rolling. Some later authors ascribed to him a pot belly and bowlegs. Aristophanes compared his walk to the strut of a waterfowl.

Socrates' mental characteristics were also striking. From his childhood, he claimed to be attended by a *daimonion*, which has been variously translated as a 'mysterious voice', a 'supernatural sign', or a 'guardian spirit'. The sign manifested itself in no particular pattern and often on trivial occasions; it always took the form of a sudden inhibition. Socrates' experience taught him that neglect of its guidance generally led to unpleasant consequences. The importance of the sign for us is that it indicates something of Socrates' visionary temperament, which is also exemplified by his tendency to engage in long periods of contemplation, as if in a kind of trance or ecstasy.

The mystical element of Socrates' character is balanced by the down-to-earth. According to Plato, he was possessed of an 'obstinate rationality' which was coupled with a good sense of humour. He is also said by some of Plato's characters to have an 'habitual irony'; this is generally taken to be an unattractive quality, indicative of a man who evades his responsibilities by self-deprecation.

Chaerephon, an ardent admirer of Socrates, made a visit to Delphi and asked the oracle if anyone in Greece was wiser than Socrates. The Pythia told him there was none. After hearing of this, Socrates, according to Plato, set out to refute the oracle and thus began his campaign of questioning conventional wisdom, claiming himself to be ignorant. In spite of this, he found the oracle to be right. Everyone he consulted was more ignorant than he: they thought they knew but they knew nothing, whereas Socrates at least knew that he knew nothing. From this time on, we find that he is a man with a mission. His charge is to convince men of their ignorance and to encourage that which is most important: 'tending their own souls' so as to 'make them as good as possible'.

From the time Socrates was about 38, Athens had been engaged in the Peloponnesian War; he left Athens only when on military service. Plato speaks of his involvement in three campaigns: the siege of Potidaea in 431 – 430; Delium in 424, where he served as a heavy-armed infantryman (*hoplite*); and after Amphipolis in 422. He had an excellent record as a fighting man, and his bravery is often noted.

Although he avoided politics and was critical of the Athenian democracy, we find him as president of the Assembly in 406 when a motion was raised to execute the generals who had abandoned ships and survivors after the victory at Arginusae; he flatly refused to consider the motion because of its illegality.

In 404 – 403, a revolution saw the establishment of the oligarchy of the Thirty Tyrants. Even though some of Socrates' acquaintances (Critias and Charmides) numbered among the Thirty, he disassociated himself from their activities. After a counterrevolution restored democracy to Athens, the new democrats displayed moderation in their dealings with those who had previously been their oppressors. Some minor purges did, however, take place. Socrates may have been an unfortunate victim of one such action. It may be that it was Socrates' persistent criticism of the political system and his relationship with men such as Critias, who had proved himself to be a traitor as a member of the Thirty, that brought about his downfall. The general charge brought against Socrates was *asebeia*, impiety, and the specific indictment was teaching strange gods and corrupting the youth. It is more likely, however, that his accuser, Meletus, was not really concerned with these religious and moral positions but was a foolish, but probably sincere, stooge manipulated by Anytus and Lycon, Meletus' fellow accusers, who had suffered at the hands of the Thirty. There is, however, no strong evidence to show either that the charges had substance or that political motivation was the real reason for the trial.

Socrates was charged, tried, and condemned to death. The Athenians did not particularly like execution, and there were a number of alternatives, one of which was exile. Socrates refused any compromise and drank a cup of poison hemlock in 399.

Socrates left nothing written behind. Most of what we know of his thought comes from the works of his disciple Plato. By writing in the dialogue form with Socrates usually cast as the main character and at the same time leaving himself out of the picture, Plato made it almost impossible to know how far what is ascribed to Socrates in a Platonic dialogue actually represents the views of the historic Socrates.

Socrates' views on ethics may best be understood in the context of the three Socratic paradoxes: virtue is wisdom or knowledge; no-one does evil intentionally; all virtues are one. These all point in the same direction. What is it, however, that makes them paradoxes? One main feature is that they all seem to state what is, as a matter of fact, false. They therefore become paradoxes by being interpreted as empirical statements. They are, each of them, general statements about virtue and clarification of anyone of them is clarification the other two. So, for example, if evil-doing is due to a lack of knowledge, then 'virtue is knowledge' is elliptical for that paradox. But what sort of knowledge are we talking about?

The Sophists (although we must be careful here: there was no one sophistical view *per se*), and many modern-day Sophists, claim that virtue is not knowledge if what is meant is that our knowing what virtue is entails agreement on what it is; because there is no agreement. The Sophists thought that there could be agreement of the conventional kind about virtue, but such agreement might make possible completely different views about it. The relativistic sophists thought that justice, for example, might vary from state to state and from city to city: there could be an Athenian view of justice which differed from a Spartan one.

In the *Republic* (505df), when searching for an understanding of the Good, we are given a simile (which Plato later develops into the simile of the Cave) in which we get a vague apprehension of what the Good is by considering the cause of vision and growth in the sensible world: the sun. In like manner, the Good is the cause of being and knowledge in the sensible world though it is not being or knowledge itself. Indeed, the Good outstrips them in its glory and power. In fact, Goodness itself is so mysterious that it appears to come by divine favour (*theia moira*), which I take to explain why those who are virtuous, who have knowledge, can give no account of it and cannot even tell what it is except to say that it is Goodness beyond virtue; that it is that by which all virtue is judged. In the *Phaedo* (82a), Socrates describes this Goodness as a 'philosophic goodness' (*philosophike arete*) and distinguishes it from popular goodness (*demotike arete*), doubtless the 'goodness' of the sophists. It is the former alone that is knowledge. This knowledge *is* virtue and belongs to the soul so that it is impossible for the virtuous man to do evil intentionally.

Socrates wants to say that the difference between Good and evil is independent of our agreement about the difference. Socrates' problem is: how can you point to the difference if there is no convention which decides what the difference is? So, if virtue is knowledge, as the Socratic paradox states, then the knowledge that it gives of the difference that there is between Good and evil does not rest on convention; this applies also to the unity of virtue and to the claim that it is better to suffer evil than to do it (or that no-one does evil intentionally).

That no-one does evil intentionally, when stated empirically, is patently false. But what Socrates means is: only if there is a definite distinction between Good and evil and a recognition of this difference, will it make sense to say that, for example, murder is wrong.

Iris Murdoch says:

'What [Plato] does suggest is that we work with the idea of ... a hierarchy in so far as we introduce order into our conceptions of the world through our apprehension of Good... Plato's image [of the sun as the Good] implies that complete unity is not seen until one has reached the summit, but moral advance carries with it intuitions of unity which are increasingly less misleading. As we deepen our notions of the virtues we introduce relationship and hierarchy. Courage, which seemed at first to be something on its own, a sort of specialised daring of the spirit, is now seen to be a particular operation of wisdom and love.'[6]

So, the important distinction is that between particular, individual desires, which according to Socrates may be good or evil, and the general desire for the Good which is not a particular desire (i.e. its object is not particular) but a desire which is a standard of judgement for all particular desires. It has been called an absolute Goodness which for Socrates is a mystery, something of which he is ignorant. The Form of the Good, for Plato, is not something for which we aim; it is that in the light of which all our aims are judged. The Good, for Plato, is beyond time, it is unchanging, it is *sui generis.* Here is the difference between Aristotle and Plato: the difference between virtue and Goodness beyond virtue.

The knowledge with which Socrates equates virtue, when he rejected the mention of particular instances of things done or not done as relevant to an understanding of the nature of virtue, is thus akin to Kant's (Immanuel Kant, 1724 – 1804) *pure reason.* As a synonym for 'pure reason' Kant used the term '*a priori* reason' and the significance of these terms is to be found primarily in what they deny. Pure reason is that which contains no admixture of the empirical. It is not, to use the Platonic mode of expression, knowledge of the world of many particulars, but knowledge of one thing only – the Form of the Good.

When we give empirical examples of virtues, say, honouring parents, then the examples we give are determined by convention in the sense that we have decided to call certain kinds of virtuous actions by certain names; this leads us to think of them as different and to forget what it is they have in common, Murdoch's hierarchy. The problem, however, is precisely in saying what it is they have in common. If we attempt this, we run into difficulty simply because we are attempting to say something that is not amenable to the conventions of that kind of language which we use to state what is the case. For example, the statement 'all virtues are one' is not a description of virtue as the statement 'courage is a virtue' can be. We could imagine someone making a mistake with regard to 'courage is a virtue'. She might, for instance, call a just act courageous if she did not know how we use the word 'just', and that would be mistaken convention; but she would still regard the act as virtuous.

So the question is: what is recognising something as virtue at all? The recognition is independent of any convention. It depends on the absolute distinction between what is virtue and what is not. But this is no longer to make an empirical judgement, but a moral one. Thus, we can also make sense of 'no one does evil intentionally'. In the latter, Socrates is referring not to what is possible or impossible as a matter of fact; he is referring to what is logically impossible: that is, the fact that if it makes sense for me to say that I am doing wrong then I must know that what I am doing is wrong. He contends that the Good is desired because it is Good, not that it is good because it is desired. Socrates is not making some kind of inductive generalisation about men's desires; he is talking about what is desired, the Good, independently of any particular desires.

The consequentialists of Socrates' day sanctioned doing evil: they let in propositions like 'this is an evil thing to do but I'm justified in doing it' or 'it is evil but I must do it'. Socrates would have regarded these as crooked propositions: 'it is evil but I must do it' means 'I must not do it but I must do it', a *non sequitur*.

The desire for the Good is what Socrates refers to in the *Apology* when he says:

'I say the same to everyone I meet... I know that this is the command of God; and I believe that to this day no greater good has ever happened in the state than my service to God. For I do nothing but go around persuading, old and young alike, not to take thought for your persons or your properties but first and chiefly to care about the greatest improvement of your soul' (30a).

Again, compare Murdoch:

'Asking what good is is not like asking what Truth or what Courage is, since in explaining the latter the idea of Good must enter in, it is that in the light of which the explanation must proceed. "True courage is..." And if we try to define Good as x we have to add that we mean a good x. If we say that Good is Reason we have to talk about good judgement. If we say that Good is love we have to explain that there are different kinds of love. Even the concept of Truth has its ambiguities and it is really only of Good that we can say "it is the trial of itself and needs no other touch".[7]

It is also connected with what Socrates says in the *Apology* about ignorance. This is not just irony as is often claimed: Socrates' intention is to point out that knowledge about the Good is a form of ignorance. He says this in order to show that it cannot be knowledge as it is generally understood, as it is presented by the Sophists. It becomes ironic because Socrates knows that those to whom it is addressed will suppose that the knowledge he disclaims is of such a kind that one could give an account of it in similar terms to those in which other forms of knowledge could be described. So they will not understand his ignorance, and will imagine that it is feigned. This is the point of the comparison of knowledge of virtue with those forms of knowledge that we find in the various skills. Socrates often made the comparison between virtue and the skills or crafts (*technai*), and, unhelpfully one might think. But there are some aspects of this comparison which may be seen as legitimate: the *technai* can be taught by masters of the respective arts and crafts but there are no masters who can, in like manner, teach virtue. For the masters of crafts, knowledge is something independent of the possessor it; that means that it can be learned and taught. Rather we may say it is knowledge to which the distinction made by Aristotle between potential and actual knowledge applies. The knowledge becomes actual in its application – it is in this sense practical knowledge. But this distinction does not apply to knowledge of virtue. Knowing what virtue is in this sense is identical with *being* good – that is, virtue *is* the knowledge; it is *being* virtuous. And that is why Socrates claimed to be ignorant; for in the sense in which knowledge was thought of, as being knowledge of something particular, knowing what virtue is could not be anything of the sort. True wisdom lies in knowing Good and evil and this knowledge is identical with virtue. Socrates knows the difference between Good and evil but not why there is this difference. The Good is, essentially, transcendent and, as such, mysterious.

We cannot give a reason for the necessity of being virtuous which is something different from knowing that virtue is necessary. Our knowledge of virtue is only knowledge of the necessity of being virtuous itself and not knowledge of a kind which gives a reason for its necessity.

Cave Life

Plato explains this by means of the simile of the

cave. In the *Republic* Book VII, we find a cave where chained prisoners are unable to see anything but moving shadows which they mistake for reality. For Plato, it is the world outside the cave which provides the real light, the Form of the Good. We get an apprehension of the Good only by seeing the world, or some of the things that are in the world, in a certain light. And while we can turn in its direction, we do not ourselves supply the light: the Good provides the light. Plato recognised that the problem of spurious semblances – the mistaken shadows of the cave – ran right through ethics. In the cave, relative light is taken for absolute light; images gyrate and are taken for reality and made the subject of the consequentialist style of science. There is an interest in forecasting outcomes and planning accordingly. Some people are adept at this. Getting to be adept at it is the limit of what they can achieve, and so, in a way, they reach the absolute – but only by the standards of the cave.

The knowledge that there is of the difference between Good and evil must be gained, without teaching, by every person for herself. If a person does see the difference and makes this recognition a guiding principle in her life then she is, in Socrates' words, caring for her soul.

Consequentialists make light of good and evil as absolute properties; they regard them as nothing more than agents working towards some deal. But under a superordinate purpose, there is a subordinate conjunction of those embroiled in the situation, what they do, and what are the effects of their actions. For example, and to paraphrase Gaita, if a man kills another man, actions with an evil shape to them do not *just happen* to flow from him and they do not *just happen* to have evil consequences. Indeed, the evil-doer gets what he chooses: he makes himself and evil-doer. A person who commits murder makes himself a murderer. It is better to suffer evil than to do it.

Actions do not originate in and come out of the human beings in the way that sunlight originates in and is emitted by the sun. Generally speaking, as Aristotle said, a human being is in her actions somewhat as a bird is in flight. The relation between action and perception should not therefore be regarded as a contingent one. For Plato it is necessary: what must be understood is what makes it possible for humans to call not some particular thing, but anything, Good independent of human opinion. It is seeing the difference between Good and evil and making this recognition a guiding principle in one's life. And this, for Socrates, amounts to caring for one's soul.

In the *Apology* (42a), Socrates says:

'But it is necessary for you, my judges, to face death with good hope and to be certain of this one thing at least – that no evil can befall an upright man either in life or death, and that this life is in the hands of God. For now the hour has come for me to die. You will go on living. Which is the better fate is known to no-one except God.'

For Socrates, death is not the worst of evils, wickedness is:

'It is not hard to escape death; it is much more difficult to escape wickedness; for that runs faster than death.' (39a)

Ultimately, this is for Socrates, as it must be for us all, a matter of faith.

In her paper *Modern Moral Philosophy*[8], Elizabeth Anscombe said that anyone who thought in advance that it may be permissible in certain circumstances judicially to punish a person known to be innocent, showed a corrupt mind. If she is right, then consequentialism, and with it most modern moral philosophy, is corrupt.

This need not, of course, be a bar to doing moral philosophy: even the most corrupt mind might produce insights inspired by truth just as morally corrupt artists might produce works of incomparable beauty.

But this simply points to the difference between moral, and particularly academic, philosophy and the ethical life as exemplified by Socrates. For Socrates there could be no distinction between doing philosophy and desiring the Good. As Gaita says:

'... the problem of finding a style or a voice in moral philosophy is not simply a consequence of the problematical relation between moral philosophy and subjects other than philosophy... The difficulty also arises from the fact that moral philosophy has, within itself and to a greater degree than other parts of philosophy, the tension between philosophy as a subject and philosophy as Socrates did it.'[9]

Conclusions must, Socrates tries still to teach us, be owned and lived. We should not, as Jesus taught, be like the hypocrites who pray thus and so in the synagogues.

The Platonic, some of the Kantian and the Kierkegaardian conception of morality, with its reference to *Forms*, to *Noumena* and to the *Eternal*, may be called the religious or absolute conception of morality. It is characteristic of religious utterances that they should require an attitude to the world to be expressed by speaking of something beyond, or something which transcends, the world. The only appropriate commitment to the transcendent is an absolute commitment; to give anything less is to trivialise the transcendent, to lose a proper sense of proportion. But notice here that an absolute conception of Good and evil is not dependent on anything religious; it need not arise from religion.

As Murdoch says:

'Art... so far as from being a playful diversion of the human race, is the place of its most fundamental insight, and the centre to which the more uncertain steps of metaphysics must constantly return.

'I think the "machinery of salvation" (if it exists) is essentially the same for all. There is no complicated secret doctrine. We are all capable of criticising, modifying and extending the area of strict obligation which we have inherited. Good is non-representable and indefinable. We are all moral and equally at the mercy of necessity and chance. These are the true aspects in which all men are brothers.'[10]

As Murdoch suggests, the Good, being transcendent and absolute, is not something inferred from its various instances or which is empirically discovered. We do not stumble over moral facts. One looks inward and in touching the eternal one acts for eternity's sake, without respect for the consequences; or, paraphrasing Kant: always treat humanity, including yourself, as an end, never as a means (although this is by no means without serious difficulties). As Murdoch says:

'Good, not will, is transcendent. Will is the natural energy of the psyche which is sometimes employable for a worthy purpose. Good is the focus of attention when an intent to be virtuous coexists (as perhaps it almost always does) with some unclarity of vision. Here... beauty appears as the visible and accessible aspect of the Good. The Good itself is not visible.'[11]

The rejection of the relative ends of the utilitarians and the Aristotelians must be accomplished through action, 'a period of striving', as Kierkegaard calls it.

The sort of reasoning involved in ethical action has nothing to do with getting up in the morning and putting one's clothes on or with running a business; it has nothing to do with coping with the contingent; it is not some sort of skill that can be got up at a management course, or acquired by experience. It is not, *pace* Aristotle, to do with means securing ends. For Murdoch, Kant, Kierkegaard, Plato and Socrates it has nothing to do with the vicissitudes of the daily round; it is concentrated, rather, on the eternal, the absolute.

Kant refused to instantiate instances of the categorical imperative. Kierkegaard eschewed the temporal. And Plato, in equating virtue with knowledge, refused to accept that particular instances of good or bad actions were relevant to the nature of virtue. These are religious, or I would prefer to say spiritual, conceptions of reality. For Plato, the unworldly, formal unity of virtue is an inward unity: *dikaiosune* (righteousness/justice) is a state of the soul; this inwardness on which all true ethical understanding is based is that which touches the eternal. For Kierkegaard, Truth is subjectivity. By this he does not mean what Hume or Locke meant. For Kierkegaard, as for Kant and Plato, the Eternal – by whatever expression: Forms, the Good, the Noumenal, etc. – are cardinal qualifications of the distinction between the inner and outer life in relation to ethics.

The views of morality which are guided by the pragmatic, the utility of things, the consequences, the intentions, all these, whose attractiveness appears to rest in some kind of teleological means to ends, fail.

Such failure is evident when one compares the accounting procedures of utilitarianism with the unconditionality of the views of Plato: for example, Socrates says that it is worse to do harm than to suffer it (*Gorgias* 469b). How can this be? asks Polus, for whom better and worse makes sense only in terms of expediency. But for Socrates there is another kind of 'better' operating; this is not a matter of convention but is something to do with the inner life of which external circumstances cannot deprive one (this is why the Psalmist could bless God even though he was walking through the valley of the shadow of death; and this is why Job could bless a God who gives *and* who takes away; and this is why Socrates could face death with equanimity: a relation with the eternal is independent of the way things happen to go in the world).

Wittgenstein understood this distinction:

'If for instance, I say this is a good chair, this means that the chair serves a certain predetermined purpose; and the word "good" here has only meaning so far as this purpose has been previously fixed upon. In fact, the word "good" in the relative sense simply means coming up to a predetermined standard. Thus when we say that this man is a good pianist we mean that he can play pieces of a certain degree of difficulty with a certain degree of dexterity. And similarly if I say that it is *important* for me not to catch a cold, I mean that catching a cold produces certain describable disturbances in my life; and if I say that this is the *right* road, I mean that it's the right road relative to a certain goal. Used in this way these expressions don't present any difficult or deep problems. But this is not how ethics uses them!

'Supposing that I could play tennis and one of you saw me playing and said "well, you play pretty badly" and suppose I answered "I know I'm playing badly but I don't want to play any better", all the other man could say would be "Ah, then that's all right". But suppose I told one of you a preposterous lie, and he came up to me and said "You're behaving like a beast" and then I were to say "I know I behave badly, but then I don't want to behave any better", could he then say "Ah, then

235

that's all right"? Certainly not! He would say "Well, you *ought* to want to behave better". Here you have an absolute value of judgement, whereas the first one was of relative judgement.'[12]

The 'Science' of Morality

The search for a scientific foundation of morality is not new: its progenitors, following Bacon's challenge to the old Scholastic model, were Hobbes and Locke and, of course, Hume. With Hume's sentimentalism as his model, Bentham developed his principles of utility, using the 'felicific calculus': attempting to quantify the value, and classify the kinds, of pleasure and pain which might be used to calculate the extent of happiness.

These early varieties of naturalism now present themselves in new guises: E.O. Wilson's fearless though naive philosophising in his sociobiology (which has since transmogrified into evolutionary psychology), primatology, evolutionary biology, neuroscience and social psychology: all burgeoning fields of research used to get at what is assumed to be the science behind morality.

For example: I mentioned above Philippa Foot's 'LA Trolley Case'. Functional magnetic resonance imaging (fMRI) has been used to scan subjects considering the trolley case and the related 'footbridge case' (essentially, the same as the trolley case except that instead of the lever being pulled to divert the trolley from the five to the one, a large man, if pushed from the footbridge above the oncoming trolley car will prevent the death of the five). fMRI scans during the presentation of the two cases show that there is increased neural activity in the dorsolateral prefrontal cortex during the lever-switch case but increased neural activity in the ventromedial prefrontal cortex during the footbridge case. In other words, different parts of the brain predominate in the two different cases. Doubtless, this exercise indicates a correlation between brain activity and moral thought processes. There is, however, a tendency among these researchers wrongly to conflate such descriptivism with the prescriptive nature of ethics: morality seen as a manifestation of psychology. Such neuroscientific studies have no value when it comes to understanding good and evil, right and wrong and how one should live. These findings amount to little more than new empirical insights into what we've known at least since Hume: that moral judgement has an emotional component; that it is, at times, intuitive; that it involves, at times, conscious calculation. And now we know that these things can be plotted in the brain.

The attempts of these scientists to blur the line between description and prescription, between Gray's derided 'is' and 'ought', gives no credence to claims of the discovery of a scientific foundation for morality.

Much of the impetus for such a discovery is fostered by such institutions as John Brockman's Edge Foundation Inc.[13] whose goal is to refashion public culture, including morality, in the light of science. Brockman is the literary agent for Steven Pinker and Richard Dawkins, among others. The Edge Foundation is just one of many public bodies given to a scientific naturalism of morality. Closer to home is the Cambridge Moral Psychology Research Group[14], and interest in the scientific moral quest is worldwide and growing. But these endeavours bring us no closer to knowing what we *should* do in the moral realm and often amount to moral nihilism.

GE Moore (in *Principia Ethica*, 1903) exposed this deficiency in his contention that goodness cannot be a natural property. Moore's 'naturalistic fallacy' denies the validity of deriving ethical conclusions from non-ethical premises: taking a naturalistic property to be the meaning of the term 'good'. But even if the naturalistic property in question, say, 'highly evolved', happens to coincide with goodness, that doesn't show that the meaning of 'goodness' *is* the naturalistic property: we can still ask of 'highly evolved' if it is good. As Murdoch argues: 'Good' resists analysis. While Moore's 'open question argument' has some force, it is not without problems.

There will never be a scientific basis for morality.

Clearly it is possible to distinguish between different elements of the good, or indeed the bad; we all do this kind of thing daily. But understanding what it is that makes these different elements of the Good or bad is not something one does every day. While I might, under cross-examination, be able to give further details of the Good and even to draw comparisons between this good and that, I am hardly able to expatiate upon what the Good or the bad, independently of these descriptors, is. I simply would have no means of answering such a demand. I know the Good and the bad; I have no problem with this. But how can I tell what it is?

I can think of a whole range of answers to this question which are entirely conceptually inappropriate (Aristotle, J.S. Mill, Rawls, etc.). These have all got things precisely backwards: attempting to explain the absolute by inferences from its instances. They are, all of them, wrong: knowing the Good, for example, is not something that can be got up from a book. As D.Z. Phillips has argued: instead of it being the case that anything can come to have value by means of being related to a superordinate purpose, purposes that are not subordinate to other purposes call for understanding from the standpoint of absolute value – just as they do when they are merely subordinate.[15]

It is true, absolutely true, that either *p* or *not p*; this is, in one sense, trivial. There are different kinds of absolute judgements: some relate to the recognition that something is Good or evil. Such a recognition is not, at times, a judgement: it confers nothing. Why this Goodness is what it is or why it should be there at all – it's quiddity – is a mystery; a thought consequentialists cannot bear. To attempt to explain absolute values is to relativize them. One can't explain Goodness; one just knows it. But more than that: I would reject any attempt to explain it.

In the absence of absolute conceptions, there can be nothing profound in ethics. Consequentialist explanations of ethics impede any attempt to ascribe absolute value to actions; that they might, in their own right, be Good or evil. We are always presented, rather tediously, with the 'greatest happiness' (whatever that is supposed to mean. Bentham's 'hedonistic' or 'felicific calculus' is even more mysterious) or the consequences, or the actor's intentions, or... But I suggest we consider, with Murdoch, 'Good as absolute, above courage and generosity and all the plural virtues, is to be seen as unshadowed and separate, a pure source, the principle which creatively relates the virtues to each other in our moral lives.'[16]

Evil consequences are internal to the nature of evil actions. Where there is a significance for

Good or evil, agent, action and consequences are all components; they are part of the whole; they are, as Plato would say, one. Gray contends that absolutism in ethics depends on belief in God. But why must one believe in a God or gods to hold a belief in the transcendence of the Good? It is not necessary to invoke the Deity to believe in, as Iris Murdoch calls it, 'the Sovereignty of Good'.

Notes:

1. p. 45, *Seven Types of Atheism*, Allen Lane, 2018.
2. 'Moral and Legal Obligation, in *The Journal of Philosophy*, Vol. LXXII, No. 12, 1975.
3. pp. 88-89, *Straw Dogs,* Granta, 2002.
4. p. 112, *Straw Dogs.*
5. p. 89, *The Sovereignty of Good*, Routledge, 2001.
6. pp. 92-93, *op. cit.*
7. pp. 95-96, *op. cit.*
8. *Philosophy*, Vol. 33, No. 124.
9. pp. 18-19, *Good and Evil*, Routledge, 2nd ed., 2004.
10. pp. 71-72, *op. cit.*
11. p. 68, *op. cit.*
12. *Philosophical Review,* Vol. 74, No. 1, 1965.
13. www.edge.org
14. www.phil.cam.ac.uk/seminars-phil/moral-psychology
15. See, e.g., 'Some Limits to Moral Endeavour' in *Through a Darkening Glass,*

Blackwell, 1982.
16. p. 507, *Metaphysics as a Guide to Morals*, Chatto & Windus, 1992.

18
Death

William James considered immortality to be a *sine qua non* in religious life: 'Religion, in fact, for the great majority of our own race means immortality, and nothing else. God is the producer of immortality; and whoever has doubts of immortality is written down as an atheist without farther trial'.[1]

In the *Tractatus Logico-Philosophicus*, Wittgenstein says: 'Death is not an event in life. We do not live to experience death... our life has no end in just the way in which our visual field has no limits' (6.4311).

Will I survive my death? Am I anything other than my body? What is the nature of the relationship between my mind and my body? These questions contain non-religious presuppositions involved in considerations of immortality.

'The notion of the self is not the notion of an inner substance, necessarily private, whose existence and nature we must guess or infer from bodily behaviour which is but a pale reflection of the reality behind it. Persons are not mysterious entities that we never meet directly or have direct knowledge of.'[2]

D.Z. Phillips goes on to argue that if one can show that the possibility of having some kind of inner life depends on there being common activities in a common language, then any attempt to identify the essence of the self – mind, soul, spirit, call it what you will – with an inner substance divorced from such connections can be shown to be radically confused. He is right.

While it is the case that not one cell in my body now is a cell that was in my body as a child, what links me with my past is nothing but bodily continuity. Without this bodily continuity or, indeed, without the body, there can be no content whatever in the notion of personal identity; this is *one* reason why the Hindu doctrine of *samsara* (the transmigration of souls) is a nonsense.

Understanding what is meant by 'survives' and what is meant by 'death' means one is at a loss to understand what it means to ask: 'Will I survive my death?'

Is it possible to believe in the 'immortality of the soul' not entailing the survival of one's death?

When I was a teenager, I was taken to the Sydney Cricket Ground to an open-air rally conducted by the American evangelist Billy Graham. He told the story of a sparrow flying with a grain of sand in its beak to the moon, depositing it on the moon and returning to the earth. By the time it has removed every grain of sand from earth and put it on the moon, 'It's only breakfast time in heaven', said Mr Graham. As a 14-year-old, I found this odd.

If one construes eternity – as in 'eternal life' – as earthly time extended to infinite duration, then one has failed to understand that eternity is qualitatively different; that it is *not* of this world.

We can understand this by reference to Plato's *Phaedo*, the dialogue about immortality, telling of the discussion between Socrates and his disciples on the night before he drank the poison hemlock. Here Socrates is conversing with Simmias (64 d-e):

Socrates: Do you think a true philosopher would think much of the cares of the body – I mean such as the possession of fine clothes and shoes and other personal adornments? Do you think you would care about them or despise them, except so far as it is necessary to have them?
Simmias: I think the true philosopher would despise them.
Socrates: Altogether, then, you think that such a man would not devote himself to the body, but would, so far as he was able, turn away from the body and concern himself with the soul.

Here Plato is suggesting that to cleanse one's soul we must turn from the temporal to the eternal. Shortly afterwards, he goes on to speak of *absolute* justice, beauty, truth and wisdom and so on.

The man who is concerned with the temporal is subject to his desires and passions and these determine the way he behaves. Such a man, we are told, 'shall never attain the truth' because he is a 'slave to (bodily) service' who 'lacks order in his soul'.

Eternal life is the reality of goodness, the *Idea*, as Plato would have it, in terms of which human life is judged.

Talk of a man's soul is in fact talk about the way he lives his life and this relation is not a contingent one.

Phillips says:

'Talk about the soul... is not talk about some strange sort of "thing". On the contrary, it is a kind of talk bound up with certain moral or religious reflections a man may make on the life he is leading. Once this is recognised, once one ceases to think of the soul as a thing, as some kind of incorporeal substance, one can be brought to see that in certain contexts talk about the soul is a way of talking about human beings.'[3]

This is so, in part, for Plato also: the notions of absolute goodness, etc. constitute eternal life, the life of the good, of truth, to which the soul aspires.

Talk of the immortality of the soul can thus be seen to be other than disquisitions on whether one survives one's death; it can be seen to be an attempt to place eternal life in a moral or religious context. Thus eternity ceases to be life of infinite duration but, as with Plato's absolutes, a means by which *this* life is judged, is seen as *sub species aeternitatis*. As Wittgenstein says: 'Not only is there no guarantee of the temporal immortality of the human soul, that is to say of its eternal survival after death; but, in any case, this assumption completely fails to accomplish the purpose for which it has always been intended. Or is some riddle solved by my surviving forever? Is not this eternal life itself as much of a riddle as our present life? The solution of the riddle of life in space and time lies *outside* space and time' (6.4312).

Indeed, Phillips says: 'In learning by contemplation, attention, renunciation, what forgiving, thanking, loving, etc. mean in these contexts, the believer is participating in the reality of God; *this is what we mean by God's reality*'.[4]

Phillips notes that a man may actually visualise his family, most of whom are dead, embracing each other in a reunion after death. But who is it that entertains these pictures literally? Who ponders them and builds up details, as if a kind of fantasy? Such ruminations, and questions arising from them, are not just awkward; they are trivial. But such pictures equally may have an ethical and religious role in a person's life.[5]

As we have seen, William James thought immortality vital to the religious life and this is used by some to induce expectations of living a virtuous life. But, *caveat emptor*: JS Mill warns that we should be careful what we wish for:

'It is not only possible but probable that in a higher, and above all, a happier condition of human life, not annihilation but immortality may be the burdensome idea; and that human nature, though pleased with the present, and by no means impatient to quit it, would find comfort and not sadness in the thought that it is not chained through eternity to a conscious existence which it cannot be assured that it will always wish to preserve.'[6]

Notes:

1. p. 524, *The Varieties of Religious Experience.*
2. p. 5, *Death and Immortality,* Macmillan, 1970.
3. pp. 44-45, *op. cit.*
4. p. 55, *op. cit.*
5. p. 68, *op. cit.*
6. p. 122, *Three Essays*, Longman, 1887.

Postscript

Causes rarely provide meanings. And, as we have seen, attempts to trace faith to its roots inevitably end in failure. But religion is a strange sediment in human consciousness – which itself might have an evolutionary cause - and trying to understand it is a worthy enterprise. Unbelief is, also inevitably, a negative exercise, but only if it is seen as a denial of belief rather than as a vision of the world suffused with a hope and a joy in the fulness of a life lived without the transcendent; or, possibly, with an other-worldly hopelessness, as, sadly, it so often is in the atheists surveyed by John Gray in his scintillating *Seven Types of Atheism.* Western atheism has been fixated on the idea of the existence of God – the hint is in the name – but this has been its principal mistake. Religion without existential theistic claims has no need for the interminable and ultimately pointless arguments of natural theology nor for a theodicy.

To paraphrase Roger Scruton, there are plenty of religions in which the belief in the gods is a hazy and sceptical afterthought and where ritual and community are far more important than any theological doctrine, as William James also argued. The religion of ancient China was like this – that is, with the gods as an afterthought; so too was the religion of Rome. Hinduism, with many hundreds of gods, is for that reason adjacent to Buddhism, with none (Gray is right to remind us that monotheism should not be taken as our paradigm of what religion is and has been). As we have seen, religious propositional belief is a highly over-rated exercise and far from trouble-free. Religion is a source of consolation, a cure for our metaphysical loneliness, a vision of affirmation in a broken world and sometimes a crippled and corrupted vision making the world even more broken.

Of course, there is always the form, the ethics, the practice and the liturgy of belief – the stuff of the godless and god-filled religions alike. But there can never be justification; the unbelief which attacks this misguided notion is chasing a chimera. Visions of the world don't offer justifications any more than lovers do: 'Greater love hath no man than this, that a man lay down his life for his friends' (*John* 15:13). Although some visions, like some forms of Islam for example, can be utterly corrupt.

It is undoubtedly impossible to recover anything from the life of Jesus that would constitute a sufficiently sound basis for religious propositional belief, let alone for faith. But belief in its propositional sense is mostly befuddled and almost always not representative of faith. If belief, as it is most commonly understood today, is the salient criterion of the religious life, then the dim and the demented are damned. But no-one seriously believes this to be the case. Faith is not belief; faith is a virtue, like love.

A key question for belief and unbelief alike has been whether some sort of religious commitment can be sustained denuded of metaphysical content. But whether God exists or not is a trivial question and actually plays no significant role in the life of faith. Faith should be seen as a thoroughly natural phenomenon.

Gray's God-haters should not be called atheists: who is it they hate, if not God? The nuances of the visions of atheists that Gray rightly identifies show us that, at times, there may be only a slither of difference between belief and unbelief while at times there is a yawning gap of incomprehension. Metaphysical atheism is as misguided as metaphysical theism.

Belief in God, which may or may not be analogous to belief in the existence of the external world, can be seen, in classical fashion, as belief in a God who is all the *omnis*: omniscient, omnipotent, omnipresent, etc. It doesn't have to be thus: belief in God might simply be expressed as 'ultimate concern', as Tillich suggested; a commitment to something that transcends the mundane and humdrum, expressed as a hope and often mediated through art and music or in those indefinable but indispensable virtues of beauty, truth and goodness. Likewise, just as ethics may be seen as a belief in the sovereign Good, as *sui generis*, so also this commitment can form part of a vision of life otherwise called faith. And this faith might take its expression through the vision of the Christian religion, of Judaism, of atheism, etc.

Such a commitment, denuded of metaphysical elements, might be an expression of the all too human quest for meaning; a commitment to faith, hope and love. Such a commitment can also be shared by those who label their vision 'unbeliever', even if they do not share the cultus from which it arises.

Appendix
Aristotle's Theology

Aristotle was born at Stagira in northern Greece in 384 BC. His father was physician to King Amyntas II of Macedonia. At 17, he went to Athens to study under Plato. He stayed at the *Academy* for nearly 20 years until Plato's death in 348/7. On Plato's death, he is reported to have said that Plato was the man 'whom bad men have not even the right to praise, and who showed in his life and teachings how to be happy and good at the same time'.

After Plato's nephew was appointed as his successor at the Academy, Aristotle left for Assos where he may have founded a branch of the Academy. Three years later, he went to Mytilene in Lesbos and, after a short stay, in 343/2, was invited to Pella by King Philip of Macedonia to tutor his 13-year-old son Alexander, later to be called 'The Great'.

When Alexander ascended the throne in 335, Aristotle, aged 49, returned to Athens where he founded his own philosophical school, the *Lyceum*, in the north east of the city in the precincts of Apollo Lyceus; there he worked for 12 years until Alexander's death in 323.

The Athenian reaction to Macedonian suzerainty led to Aristotle being charged, as had Socrates before him, with *asebeia*, impiety. He escaped Athens, having been reported to have said, 'lest the Athenians should sin against philosophy for the second time' and went to Chalcis in Euboea where he lived on his dead mother's estate. He died the following year, in 322/1, aged 62. Aristotle had married twice and left a son, Nicomachus, by his second wife, after whom his greatest work on ethics is named.

Aristotle's main works covered metaphysics, ethics and logic but he also wrote on natural science, psychology, meteorology, anatomy, physiology, biology, epistemology, mathematics, rhetoric, aesthetics, dialectic, politics, poetry and the nature of philosophy itself. He was, arguably, one of the greatest polymaths the world has known.

Aristotle's view of the first unmoved mover is not only a result of his empirical observations. He thinks that an examination of physical motion can lead to the conclusion that there is a first mover which does not move (*Physics* 267B), but the nature of this first mover Aristotle thinks of as *mind*, not itself something deducible from empirical observation. His argument, as elegantly presented by St Thomas Aquinas in his *First Way* and translated by Anthony Kenny, goes as follows:

'The first and most obvious way is based on motion. It is certain as a matter of sense-observation that some things in this world are in motion. Now whatever is in motion is moved by something else. For nothing is in motion except insofar as it is in potentiality to the term of its motion. Something moves, on the other hand, insofar as it is in actuality. This is because to move is precisely to bring something from potentiality to actuality; but a thing cannot be brought from potentiality to actuality except by something which is itself in actuality. Thus, something which is actually hot, like fire, makes something which is potentially hot – say wood – to be actually hot: and in this way it moves and alters it. Now it is not possible for the same thing to be, at the same time and in the same respect, in actuality and in potentiality; for what is actually hot cannot simultaneously be potentially hot, though it may simultaneously be cold. So it is impossible that in the same respect and in the same manner anything should be both mover and moved, or that it should move itself. So whatever is in motion, must be moved by something else. Moreover, this something else, if it too is in motion, must itself be moved by something else, and that in turn by yet another thing. But this cannot go on forever: because if it did there would be no first mover, and consequently no other mover at all, since second movers do not move except when moved by a first mover, just as a stick does not move anything except when moved by a hand. And so we must reach a first mover which is not moved by anything: and this all men think of as God.'[1]

(Aquinas' First Way is given at greater length in his *Summa contra Gentiles* which uses a patchwork of Aristotelian passages drawn from two separate arguments in the seventh and eighth books of *Physics*, which conclude not to the existence of God but to the presence of a soul in the outermost sphere of the heavens. 'Motion', as a translation of Aquinas' *motus*, is not without problems, as is 'move' in Aristotle's Greek, which only has a transitive sense.)

Whether Aristotle made a clear-cut distinction

between physics and theology may be questionable, but there does seem to be an abrupt transition in *Metaphysics Book Lambda* from his statement that the existence of motion necessitates the existence of a first unmoved mover to his statement that the first unmoved mover is *mind*. Here we might compare Aristotle with Plato in the *Timaeus*: 'The father of this universe is a hard task to find'.

Aristotle's influence is evident in Christian and mediaeval Muslim thought with the view that theology is a systematic account of God's nature (cf. here the neo-Platonic view which says that such machinations as Aristotle's are impossible).

God, for Aristotle, is *perfect thought*. Human beings shared the divine life and the reason for this is that: 'If happiness is an activity in accordance with virtue, it is reasonable to suppose that it will be in accordance with the highest virtue; and this can only be the virtue of the best part of us' (*Nicomachean Ethics* 1177 a 11). The best part of us is, of course, mind and so, he goes on: 'The man whose activity is one of the mind and who cultivates that and keeps it in the best condition is also the man whom the gods love above all others'. Aristotle believes that the virtue of the intellectual life is superior to that of the moral life. To distinguish between intellectual and moral virtue seems to be one of the main purposes of his *Ethics*.

In chapter nine of *Book Lambda*, Aristotle's thought suffers the inevitable fate of any attempted systematic theology which essays to give an account of God's nature in analogy with human life: what we are left with is an account of human nature with certain limitations of human nature omitted. The result is a nonsense.

Aristotle treats the question of the relative merits of *mind* and *desire* as if it were a theoretical question to decide how they can be balanced against one another. For Plato, however, it is rather a question of how we can overcome *desire* when it is for what is evil and he does not distinguish the two when the desire is for the good. The relation between the two is never just a theoretical question for Plato, as it often is for Aristotle:

'Now we have already determined that the origin of all other motions is that which moves itself, and the origin of this is immovable. And we must grasp this not only generally in theory but also by reference to individuals in the world of sense, for with these in view we seek general theories, and with these we believe general theories ought to harmonise.' (*De Motu* 698 a 10)

Aristotle thought that it is possible to think of the nature of God in analogy with 'the world of sense'. In human action there are ends which human beings seek to achieve. In fact, the life of the soul is the achievement of these ends just as God is the final cause of the world.

Notes:

1. pp. 6-7, *The Five Ways,* R & KP, 1969. Kenny offers a fine assessment of 'The First Way' in this chapter.

ABOUT THE AUTHOR

Ian Walker

Ian Walker was born in Sydney, Australia but has spent most of his life in the UK. His doctorate at the University of Wales was supervised by Huw Price and DZ Phillips.

He was, for 26 years, Headmaster of one of the world's oldest schools (founded in 604 AD) and has taught in universities in the UK and the USA.

He is married to Kerrie, a mathematician turned lawyer; they have a daughter, Hilary, who lives in Sydney. Ian and Kerrie live in a small, rural village in Oxfordshire.

BOOKS BY THIS AUTHOR

Plato's Euthyphro

A commentary on the Greek text of one of Plato's early dialogues

Faith And Belief: A Philosophical Approach

An assessment of the nature of faith in the Christian tradition

The Number Of The Beast

A William Adams thriller. The series tracks the adventures of William Adams, Egyptologist and improbable detective.

Dr William Adams, an Oxford Egyptologist, and Laura Tennett find their lives under threat after the murder of Laura's boyfriend, Jeremy White, a research student whose doctorate Adams is supervising.

While the police seem to be getting nowhere in their investigation, William and Laura escape to a safe house in an attempt to decipher Jeremy's thesis which may hold a clue to his murder.

They are tracked down by a mysterious organisation operating within the Roman Catholic Church; their lives are in jeopardy as they discover a secret harboured by the Church for centuries and which threatens to destroy it.

Their travels in England and France lead them to the resting place of one of history's most important caches of religious documents, secured by an ancient sect implacably opposed to the Catholic Church. They discover both the riddle and the solution of Jeremy's death ... and so much more.

The Cylinder Of Babylon

A William Adams thriller. The series tracks the adventures of William Adams, Egyptologist and improbable detective.

An ancient clay cylinder, covered in cuneiform writing, is discovered by archeologists in Babylon, in war-torn Iraq. Prof William Adams is called from Oxford to translate the cylinder and there collaborates with Prof Ellie Green. Further spectacular and widely-publicized archaeological finds apparently confirm the history of the Bible. Terrorist activity forces the dig site to be closed and Adams and Green's lives are threatened.

Adams completes his translation of the cylinder only to find that his discovery could set the combustible world of the Middle East alight. National and international pressure to suppress Adams' findings mount as the cylinder goes missing.

In this dual-voiced narrative, we learn also of the travails of the original seventh-century BC owner of the cylinder and how it comes to be placed in the secret archive rooms built under King Nebuchadnezzar's great library.

Loved By The Gods

A William Adams thriller. Forthcoming.

A sensational discovery in outback Australia leads William Adams to investigate. With his own life threatened, he finds more than he bargained for.

Made in the USA
Columbia, SC
16 October 2023

24124010R00150